FEARLESS
AND FREE

31223154555495

FEARLESS AND FREE

A Memoir

JOSEPHINE BAKER

Translated from the French by
Anam Zafar and Sophie Lewis

Foreword by Ijeoma Oluo

An imprint of Penguin Random House LLC
1745 Broadway, New York, NY 10019
penguinrandomhouse.com

Originally published in French by Éditions Corrêa as *Mémoires* by Joséphine Baker
and Marcel Sauvage, in 1949. Reissued in French by Éditions Phébus,
in 2022. First English-language edition simultaneously published with
Vintage UK, a division of Penguin Random House Group, in 2025.

Copyright © 2022 by Éditions Phébus / Libella, Paris

Translation copyright © 2025 by Anam Zafar and Sophie Lewis

Foreword copyright © 2025 by Ijeoma Oluo

LIBRARY OF CONGRESS CATALOGING-IN-PUBLICATION DATA
has been applied for.

ISBN 9780593853696 (hardcover)
ISBN 9780593853719 (ebook)

Printed in the United States of America
1st Printing

BOOK DESIGN BY LAURA K. CORLESS

The estate of Josephine Baker and publisher gratefully acknowledge
the permission granted to reproduce the copyright material in this book.

The authorized representative in the EU for product safety and compliance is
Penguin Random House Ireland, Morrison Chambers, 32 Nassau Street,
Dublin D02 YH68, Ireland, https://eu-contact.penguin.ie.

CONTENTS

FOREWORD

Ijeoma Oluo

We didn't even mean to go to Paris. I had been invited to speak at a conference in Hamburg in 2021. I was excited about my talk and the opportunity to visit Germany for the first time. My partner and my teenage son were excited to go along with me. We were packed and ready, time had been taken off from work and school—when, suddenly, the day before we were supposed to leave, the speaking engagement was off.

We sat at home with our disappointment, our packed bags, and our newly free time and tried to figure out what to do next. I started googling cheap flights overseas and landed on a last-minute flight to Paris. I booked the flight for three people, found an affordable hotel, and that same day, we were headed to Paris for the first time in our lives.

I had expected a fun four days of exploring a new city. We would see the Eiffel Tower. We would eat a lot of croissants and cheese. We would force the teenager to spend some quality time with us. It would be lovely. Then we would return home, and life would go back to normal.

But the unexpected way we had even found ourselves in Paris should have let me know that things don't always go according to plan. First of all, the teenager refused to spend any quality time with us without acting like he was being punished—though I guess we should have been prepared for that. (Taking a teenager on vacation is a lot like trying to take a cat on vacation.) But my partner and I were not prepared for just how much at home we would feel in Paris. Not "at home" as in how we felt in Seattle, where our actual home is, but feeling a sense of home we had never felt in our actual hometown. We felt *safe* in a way we never had felt, as Black people, in the United States.

As we walked down unfamiliar streets, there was a distinct unremarkableness to our presence that was itself remarkable: nobody stared. Nobody crossed the street to avoid us. Our presence in a room did not seem to alter the atmosphere in any discernible way. Police walked by us like we were people and not threats. Store clerks treated us like we were customers who had likely entered their establishment to spend money, instead of inconveniences to ignore or possible thieves to actively surveil.

Further, there was evidence not only that we were not targeted or unwanted, but that, as Black artists (I as a writer and my partner as a musician), we were *valued*. And we were certainly not the first Black creatives to find a sense of safety and belonging in Paris. Paris's love of Black artists—particularly Black American artists—was evident everywhere. Walking through the city, you can see the love for James Baldwin, for Nina Simone, for Jean-Michel Basquiat—and you'll find the love especially for Josephine

Baker. Perhaps no Black American artist is more beloved in Paris than Baker, and her influence on French culture is still seen today, decades after her death.

My partner and I were inspired and immediately began imagining the life we could live in Paris. On our subsequent visits there, the nuances of the racism in French culture and society became more apparent to us. It became clear that even if we were not the primary targets of French racism and colonialism, these aspects were still present in France and still impacted the lives of millions of people of color (especially people of Arab and North African descent) in devastating ways.

But while thinking of living someplace where our creativity would be valued, where our humanity would be seen, where we could walk down the street and not feel the weight of the constant sense of unsafety that American anti-Blackness has always placed upon our shoulders—we couldn't help but wonder what we might be able to create in the place that Josephine Baker chose to call home.

Josephine Baker's story is just as French as it is American, while also being uniquely hers at the same time. For who else could ever have had a story like hers? The dancer, the singer, the ingénue, the scandal maker, the activist, the spy—Josephine Baker lived at least ten lives in one, and in this memoir we get to see in her own words the indefatigable spirit that brought her through it all.

Ms. Baker's funny, brilliant, stubborn, and fierce spirit shines through in these pages. The humanity of the beloved performer is at the center of this book, and her honesty and sense of self guide her words.

It is clear through her work and words that Baker was passionate about justice—justice for all lives. Her charitable work is well documented, and thousands of children benefited from her generosity. She dedicated years of her life and risked her own safety to support the Allied troops in World War II. Her home was a menagerie of animals she had rescued and adopted in her travels. Josephine Baker loved life and all that lived. And she railed against anything and anyone who sought to cause harm to others.

Baker was not a politician, but she was deeply political. Her very existence, as a Black woman entertainer in the early 1900s, was inherently political. She had to fight to get into just about every room she performed in. She fought against the injustice she encountered in her own life—even when doing so hurt her career—and against the injustice she saw being done to others. Perhaps no fight was closer to her heart than the fight against racial injustice and for Black liberation.

Having survived the terror of the post-Reconstruction American South in childhood, Baker was immensely grateful for the safety and acceptance she found in her adopted home of France. And subsequent trips to the United States to perform later in life would only serve to increase her appreciation for her life abroad— and deepen her commitment to speaking out on racial injustice in the States.

In her reflections on the racism she witnessed and experienced in the United States, Baker says she was shocked to see how abused and exploited Black people in the States still were. In her recollections, she shares her outrage and confusion over the unequal power dynamics she witnessed between Black and Jewish community members in New York City. She reflects on the living conditions of many Black tenants who were renting property from

Jewish landlords and the working conditions for many Black people employed by Jewish bosses—and she asks how one historically marginalized population could seem to be exploiting another marginalized population. Her language draws broad strokes, and she makes generalizations that require further discussion here. "Why, in an ironic twist of fate for both of them, must the poor colored people of Harlem be a punching bag for the Jews, who've forgotten their forefathers' story?" she laments.

Baker was right to be outraged, shocked, and confused by what she witnessed in Harlem. And her sentiments will not feel unfamiliar to many Black people in America. Throughout our country's history, our Black and Jewish communities have at times been pitted against each other, and at other times been united in common struggle. And so, Baker's outrage itself is not in error, but without the social and political context surrounding the power dynamics she witnessed, her conclusions and blanket statements can cause harm and contribute to bigotry and antisemitism, which I do believe Baker would have opposed. But regardless of whether my guess at Baker's intentions is correct, it is incumbent upon us to add some context for the reader to keep in mind while reading Baker's words.

In its efforts to keep non-white populations subjugated, white supremacy has a lot of tools at its disposal. One of its most powerful tools is the ability to pit marginalized populations against one another. One of the most common and effective ways it does this is to offer up relative power and privilege to some marginalized populations at the expense of others. We have seen this dynamic play out between marginalized communities as well as within them. Baker herself calls out those she labels "white

Negroes," whose proximity to whiteness through skin tone and eye color has given them relative power over darker-skinned Black people—power they abuse for their own benefit and at the expense of their kin. "These white Negroes, with their blue eyes, are the others' worst enemies, merciless traitors, crueler to their own kind than white extremists," she writes.

Many Black people in the United States have found themselves exploited by other oppressed populations who have been offered such relative power. But this power locks people into hierarchies of white supremacy and deputizes many oppressed people in the subjugation of those with whom they might otherwise stand in solidarity.

This is not exclusive to Black and Jewish power dynamics: the temptations of offers of white supremacy prove irresistible to many in several different marginalized populations. And so, while we recognize how the dynamic Baker witnessed came to be, it is important to remember that what she saw was not the whole picture. I speak not only of the analysis that is missing from her words, but also of the inaccuracy and harm in her statements about "the Jews," which could easily lead the reader to believe that this was the entire dynamic between Jewish and Black populations in New York. Throughout our communities' struggles in the United States, there have always been Jewish people who have actively rejected the overtures of white supremacy and who have refused to be made complicit in the oppression of Black people. And throughout much of the history of Black struggle for liberation in the States, there have been Jewish people who have stood with us and risked much to do so—and vice versa. Further, it is important to note that there are Jewish people (especially Jewish people of color) who will never be offered the relative privilege of proximity to whiteness and who have faced both racism and antisemitism throughout their lives.

I hope that in the years after this memoir was written and published, Baker was able to find more nuanced answers as to why she witnessed what she witnessed in New York.

We are *all* susceptible to bigotries, and we are all (still, to this day) horrifically miseducated on issues of bias and systemic oppression of all forms. It is, unfortunately, a part of the human experience of our deeply flawed systems. And so, while we are each responsible for the harm our words or actions may cause (even in the long years after our deaths), we are not solely responsible for that harm and are not unique in it. I can see Baker's humanity—as I hope to see yours and my own—as complex, flawed, and, until her very last day, a beautiful work in progress.

Josephine Baker is so many things in this book. Most surprising to me is how very *funny* she is. While reading, I found myself laughing out loud multiple times at her easy, smart humor. Baker loved to laugh and didn't seem to want to pass up the opportunity to have fun. She was loved and adored by millions and, by many measures, lived a life of great privilege at the height of her fame. But a lot of what she had was hard fought for every step of the way, sometimes in the face of devastating hardship, some of which she makes clear in her own words. Baker makes no attempt to hide her heartbreak and outrage over the injustice she and others faced, yet her steadfast dedication to joy is also clear. This was a woman determined, against all odds, to thrive. If you have ever wondered what the secret to Baker's groundbreaking success was, her fierce and absolute *will* to live life as freely and joyfully as possible can easily be seen as one of its most vital components.

In reading these pages, I felt privileged to be able to experience the intimacy of Baker's words and her story. It has been enlightening, entertaining, fascinating, and, at times, frustrating. In short: in these pages, you will find a life, an extraordinary life, lived to the fullest, for better or worse.

Reader, I hope in these amazing stories from the life of a Black girl from St. Louis who ran away to Paris as a teenager and conquered the world, you will be able to borrow some of her abundant boldness and ask what you may do in the world with this little life we've each been granted.

FEARLESS
AND FREE

INTRODUCTION

Marcel Sauvage

Mademoiselle Josephine Baker burst into laughter when, the first time we met in private in late 1926, I suggested the idea of her writing her memoirs.

She had just turned twenty years old and was living in two large rooms in a peaceful guesthouse near Parc Monceau in Paris.

Midday.

Josephine Baker was still asleep.

"Oh, don't worry, you were right to wake me!" she said, jumping over a small bench. "Please, take a seat."

This all happened in English because Mademoiselle Baker did not yet know French—except for a few words, such as "poor fellow," "gramophone" and "darling," and a few others, including "bonjour," "bonbon," and "Champs-Élysées."

She was in a pink dressing gown and babouche slippers of the same color; tall, thin, agile, and inclined to laugh.

The face of a wild, mischievous, and charming young girl lit up with a laugh that showed off thirty-two strong and sparkling teeth; hair hastily slicked back with oil, plastered to her head. Her nails were silver.

"Memoirs . . . But I don't *remember* my memories yet. Let's see . . ."

I waited five minutes for the interpreter, who was running late. I looked around: some budgies in a cage, next to a bust of Louis XIV; a rag doll thumbing its nose at me from atop an Empire-style cabinet; a gramophone ready to play, further away on a small table, with a wad of one-hundred-franc notes on top.

"Paul Colin asked me to write a preface for his portfolio, *Le Tumulte Noir*," she said. "So I took a pen and, just like that, I'd written a story on two blank sheets of paper. It was funny! But I wouldn't do it again, oh no!"

"Why not?"

"My goodness, you don't know what it's like! Me, write? I'm a dancer! I love to dance, it's the only thing I like to do, and I will dance until I die."

She settled into a leather armchair, head huddled into her shoulders, eyes closed. Then she threw one of her babouche slippers into the air with a laugh.

"No, really, it's impossible. But if you'd like, I can tell you my memories, and *you* could write my memoirs. How about that?"

"We could do that."

"Okay, well, I was born on the banks of the Mississippi . . . Oh, look at my poor birds!"

Someone knocked on the door. The telephone rang. The budgies inserted seeds into Louis XIV's nose.

Josephine Baker is one of a kind.

This emerged bit by bit, strikingly from music hall and theater stages, from her dancing, her singing, her movements and her poses, and from all the mishaps revealed by the spotlights.

To be clear, these recollections were gathered for the purpose of this book, but over several meetings separated by long intervals.

The first meetings took place at a time when, having become a star in *La Revue Nègre*, Josephine Baker did not yet sing and would dance dressed in a mere belt of bananas. The meetings continued approximately twenty years later, when the American girl turned starlet and then actress and French citizen of world-wide renown sang Schubert's "Ave Maria" as a magnificently headless Mary, Queen of Scots, from the top of a grand staircase and wearing a hooped dress with a train so immense it could easily hide fifty black children.

But let's not get ahead of ourselves.

It was nearing the end of October in the year 1925. I was on my way to Genoa from Trieste, just down the coast from Nice, on board a Tripcovich cargo ship. The only officer who could speak French was the one operating the Marconi wireless telegraph. This officer would incessantly recite D'Annunzio's poetry and had been collecting different brands of rice powder, perfume bottles, and silk stockings from cities around the world.

It was nighttime. The moonlit Mediterranean was calm. We were drinking a very strong Spanish chartreuse in the chart room. Between two drags on his cigarette, the young telegraph officer turned to me and said, "In Paris these days they're showing a *Revue Nègre*: very popular. Josephine Baker: a revelation."

Sometime later, back in Marseille, I happened to be reading

an issue of the newspaper *Candide* outside a seafood bar at the
Old Port. One article in particular, written by Pierre de Régnier,
caught my eye:

AT THE CHAMPS-ÉLYSÉES:
LA REVUE NÈGRE

Much has been said about it already. Some people have
returned twice, some even six times. Others still have stood
up abruptly during a scene change and left, slamming the
door behind them, outraged by the madness, the moral
degradation and the worship of inferior deities.

The revue begins at a quarter past ten.

The whole of Paris is there, in that darkened room.

The musicians of the Negro orchestra, instruments in
hand, march single file into the darkness in front of the
pearl-gray curtain.

The curtain rises.

We are in a port at night, somewhere far away. On the
moonlit quay are cargo ships and goods—and women.
Wearing shirts, or dresses, if you wish, and tignons, they
enter one behind the other to sing a little tune. These are
the "showgirls," who, onstage, almost appear to be white—
all of them but one.

The Charleston.

At this point, a peculiar character takes very quickly
to the stage, walking with knees bent, dressed in ragged
shorts, resembling a boxer kangaroo, Sen-Sen Gum, and a
racing cyclist all at once.

This is Josephine Baker.

Is it a man? Is it a woman? Her lips are painted black,
skin the color of a banana, her already-short hair pasted to
her head as if it were dressed with caviar. Her voice is high-

pitched and she shakes with a ceaseless tremor, her body squirming like a snake or, more precisely, as if it were a living saxophone and the sounds of the orchestra were coming out of her . . . She twists around and pulls faces, crosses her eyes and puffs out her cheeks, contorts herself, does the splits and, to finish, leaves on all fours, legs stiff and rear higher than her head, like a baby giraffe.

Is she horrible, is she delightful, is she black, is she white, does she have hair or is her head painted black? Nobody knows. There is no time to find out. For here she is again, quick as a one-step tune, and she is neither woman nor dancer but something as extravagant and fleeting as music itself, the ectoplasm, so to speak, of the sounds we are hearing.

And now, the finale.

We are in a nightclub.

A barbaric dance performed by the girls and Josephine Baker. This dance, of a rare unseemliness, is a triumph of lewdness, a return to the mores of an earlier age: a declaration of love, made in silence and with the arms in the air, with a simple forward movement of the stomach and a quivering of the behind. Josephine is completely naked, with one small garland of red and blue feathers around her waist and another around her neck. The feathers flutter in time to the music, growing gradually more frenetic.

Josephine twirls in her plumage, the girls cry out, and the curtain falls to a colossal rumble of the drums and a final crash of the cymbals.[1]

I was greatly excited by this review.

Baroque-style scenery in yellow, blue, pink, and orange; extravagant costumes; exotic gyrations; freedom, fantasy, funny faces; barbaric, syncopated music; rhythmic acrobatics: an entirely unknown—or undervalued—art.

And that is precisely what it was.

In some respects, the revelation of *La Revue Nègre* paralleled that of the Ballets Russes. Both were fiercely debated. Both stirred up enthusiasm and anger. Ultimately, both established themselves.

Josephine Baker, black poetry.

I did not see *La Revue Nègre,* but I still remember the wild applause that greeted her when she returned to perform for the first time at the Folies Bergère in Paris.

"A comical nudity in bronze."

A golden body with two breasts offered to—in the frantic grip of—the spasms of desire and the delights of love.

Long, determined, frenzied legs; a shifting bottom; long and slender fingers by turns tensed and soft. An extraordinarily expressive and mobile face; gleaming eyes; plump, defined lips.

During this period, Josephine Baker—in turn light-footed and led by fate, soft and strident—performed as if she were at the mercy of the saxophones and the banjos, striking fantastical poses with a poignant precision. Her dancing, which ranged from South Carolina's Charleston to the simplest gestures, pitted instinct against civilization in a style that was caricatured yet powerful. It was said that a touch of hate was also present—a desire for revenge, perhaps, or a legitimate pride in pure animality—all quickly concealed behind parody and funny faces.

Instinct, sensual frenzy. A healthy girl presented herself, contorted herself, denied herself, and finally escaped us behind the artifices of the Old Continent. An untrammeled yet good-humored woman, she broke away from the fragility and mild-mannered charms of her sex: no frills, no niceties. In herself, however, she was self-confident, sure of the richness of her possibilities.

In the eyes of Pierre Mac Orlan, Mistinguett represented self-expression tailored for the music hall with an infinitely tragic subconscious. Josephine's initial style—jumping from one race to another, from one continent to another—revealed to us a spontaneity that "shifted lines," disrupted our ways of seeing, and reminded us of a primitive order.

She embodied, perhaps, the soul of a chemical reaction.

She laughed in the face of arteriosclerosis.

And she certainly did not assume that "leaping beauty" described by André Levinson in *Paul Valéry, Philosophe de la Danse,* classic and seasoned in all its geometry and convention, "the contrary of a dream and the absence of everything accidental."[2]

For us, Josephine Baker embodied that strange poetry that came to us in the adventure novels we had read twenty years ago.

At the same time, she remained, beneath all that turbulence and nonchalance, simultaneously the most lovable, the least pretentious, the freest, and the most enigmatic of women.

A coquette with a heart of gold.

And so, in 1926 I went to Miss Baker's house. It was around four o'clock in the afternoon, the time when her maid would wake her.

Miss Baker told stories, laughed, and performed. And I took

notes. I was only accompanied by an interpreter in the beginning, until Miss Baker knew enough French to try and speak it, which was quite entertaining—sometimes very difficult. Several visits were required, as Miss Baker didn't much enjoy remembering. She lived—her finger points down at the floor, at the present—in the present moment.

Our last interviews for the first part of these memoirs took place after midnight at the cabaret that Josephine owned on Rue Fontaine in Montmartre, while society women played tennis with paper balls and rackets over bottles of champagne to an orchestra of interchangeable brass instruments.

For a few days while I was there, I accidentally became Josephine's secretary, as well as that of the cabaret and the cabaret's revue, along with Georges Sim, who was already becoming known as Simenon, the novelist.

Between dances, Josephine would bottle-feed her goat Toute-toute.

Four years passed. Josephine traveled. Upon her return, it occurred to me to continue the memoirs, to write about what had happened since, of her adventures in Europe and America.

"Hello, bonjour, my dear, how nice of you to come and see me in my little house! Why don't you rest for a minute and then I'll show you my little dears, my chickens, my rabbits, and the tiger."

1930, a Sunday in September: Le Vésinet, the outer suburbs of Paris.

She was wearing a small, simple white dress; an overgrown

child, suntanned from her travels. She sat me down. "No, you must, you must rest a while." She, on the other hand, was restless.

The "little house" where she withdrew between the last few rehearsals at the Casino de Paris (where she was the star of the new revue *Paris Qui Remue*, "Paris Kicks Up Her Heels"), and where she loved hosting friends, was an impressive Renaissance-style villa in the middle of an enormous estate complete with woods and lawns, henhouses, tennis courts, and patches of virgin forest bordered with brambles. A small, clear river wove through ponds and meandered into waterfalls, murmuring under rustic bridges, like a stage set of a Japanese garden.

But what Josephine Baker enjoyed the most at Beau Chêne—as her estate was called—were the large orchard, the greenhouses with their exotic plants, and the kitchen garden where she would go ten times a day to watch the fruits and vegetables growing and to collect snails for her family of brown ducks.

"Look at this sweet mother rabbit, Marcel. She had eleven little ones yesterday, the poor thing."

Most of all, I looked at Miss Baker herself: the passion in her tender, spiritual face; the wonder in her eyes; her honey-colored skin and her long, persuasive fingers.

She started telling a story, then stopped.

"No, not here. In the house."

In the hallway was a fifteenth-century plumed suit of armor, a man of steel standing to attention . . .

And I went back every week, to take notes.

By now, Paris's Colonial Exposition was in full swing. Every night, Josephine sang "J'ai Deux Amours" to thunderous applause: the song written for her by Vincent Scotto at two o'clock one fine morning, while standing in a carriage entranceway.

During those restful hours in Le Vésinet, Josephine conjured up the Netherlands, Denmark, Sweden, Norway, Germany, Italy, the Americas . . .

Josephine Baker is a being of exception and an equally exceptional example of success; she has the vital qualities of intuition and an intelligence that can adapt marvelously without ever submitting.

She is not a woman of formula and etiquette.

She took up operetta to resounding success.

Michel Duran wrote:

I do not remember ever having had the opportunity to see a person onstage who is blessed with gifts as numerous and brilliant as this beautiful colored American woman.[3]

Henry Bénazet said:

Her voice, which is enriched by the medium of operetta, climbs effortlessly to the peaks of the highest notes, achieving a remarkable range and a most pure tone . . . Her onstage performance is stunning. She transitions masterfully from sentimental numbers to opera buffa.[4]

Over the same period, Josephine was starring in a film and did so to great success despite its rather simplistic structure. Writing in *Les Nouvelles Littéraires,* Alexandre Arnoux acknowledged her deep sense of character:

> *Glory and success have slightly watered down the sharpness of this popular, impulsive art. However, the Josephine Baker of today owes much to the Harlem teenager imported to Europe: the flavor of the same brutish spices burns underneath the skin of this star, now educated and softened to play more civilized tricks. Despite the lessons learned and the concessions made, she is still more than simply a performer by trade and discipline, and rather an actress of direct impact and ease, an element of nature tossed suddenly onto the stage; she is above all—though few people know it and she, herself, hardly cares—a born tragedienne, one of those women who continually exceeds the script that she reads and the stage that serves as her springboard, whose power disrupts the ordinary boundaries of acting and sounds a cosmic chord within us, responding to our need to conceive eternal types and embody them in just a few faces.[5]*

Years passed again. It was 1939: war! We saw each other nearly every day. Josephine had become a wartime godmother to more than four thousand children. She felt compelled to help. To each one, she regularly sent a parcel, a photograph, and a few kind words. Two dedicated secretaries were not enough for the job.

Every night after work, she would rush from the theater to the Gare du Nord in a taxi. She was covering the costs of a refugee reception center at this station, where the number of arrivals was growing on a daily basis. She watched over the babies and cared for the children; she handed out bottles, bread and butter, and reassuring smiles. She tried her best to comfort the grief-stricken women and the elderly. She fed them, guided them . . . and forbade anyone to speak to the press regarding her involvement in this matter.

At dawn, she would make her long way home to Le Vésinet. She made sure to say a long prayer before going to bed. She would sleep for a few hours, she would take a bath, and then she would seat herself at a table in her bedroom to write to her soldiers.

After that, on to the parcels: cigarettes, chocolate, socks, tinned food, and biscuits.

In addition, she became associated with Captain Abtey, from the Second Bureau of the General Staff, France's external military agency. Here we find her stepping forward to serve the French intelligence services.

Disaster separated us. I was in Bordeaux, then Marseille, from where I boarded a ship to North Africa after the armistice. Josephine crossed the Spanish border to Madrid, then continued to Lisbon, Gibraltar, Tangier, and Marrakesh.

It was from there that she would single-handedly yet reluctantly, over several months, lead a secret, dogged, dangerous fight against the German espionage that was spreading throughout this international zone.

In 1942, the good press of Tunis, via the pen of an editor in chief, summoned Vichy's wrath upon me because, among other things that were now unacceptable, I was Josephine Baker's historiographer.

And still I had no news from her . . .

One evening, I received a telegram from Morocco. Josephine was worn out. She was in a private clinic in Casablanca where she had to undergo several operations. Her case was most serious. She did not complain. "Keep up your spirits!" she said. "Sending love."

A postcard would arrive from time to time.

"Saved!" read the final one—and with that, Josephine, almost unrecognizable, so badly had she suffered on her small white hospital bed, threw herself back into life. Two weeks before the Allies landed in North Africa, she was on her feet at her post, smiling and ready to receive soldiers in a clinic to which she had escaped at the risk of getting killed.

General de Gaulle appreciated her services. He would soon gift her a small Cross of Lorraine, a symbol of the Free French forces. Later, he would write the preface to Major Abtey's account of her secret war, in the form of an admiring handwritten letter.[6]

Josephine Baker, acting lieutenant.

Lieutenant Baker sang "J'ai Deux Amours" in Sicily to French soldiers the day before an attack.

Lieutenant Baker sang in Egypt.

She and Germaine Sablon were the only two artists sent on official missions by the First Army to perform all over North Africa and as far as the Middle East.

It was Josephine's farewell to arms.

The Bird of the Isles had returned to us.

I was in Algiers at the time, in a clinic myself, on the operating table for the eighth time since 1915. My son, companion to "Non-épine," had joined the French Resistance in a maquis in the Alps.

Since Josephine Baker came to live in France, her life seems to have changed every five years. Every new phase has presented a most exceptional surprise, a new aspect to the artist, an elevation of her being, and a fresh awareness of her possibilities.

1925—The heyday of jazz. The Black Venus is a revelation. Josephine Baker is a curiosity, a whirlwind, a scandal of a dancer.

1930—Josephine Baker is no longer a fleeting phenomenon. She is a star at the Casino de Paris; a European star. Her voice—her birdsong—touches a vast audience.

1935—From dancing to singing, from singing to the theater and the screen. She lends her ardor, her smile, her yearnings, to Offenbach's music and Marc Allégret's cinema. Her double eloquence of body and heart make her not merely an actress but a complete artist.

1940—Nothing matters to Josephine except serving her adopted country. She is under the army's orders. This war, in her eyes, is a crusade against racist policies. She plays an unexpected and considerable role in the shadows.

1945—Enriched by singular human experience, the range of her voice is as greatly increased and purified as it is accentuated, amplified by the fire of collective and personal griefs; her movements become simpler and magnificently confident, avoiding any illusory motion; she is mindful of the exemplar, certain of an egoless mission that she undertook in a strange dialogue with herself. Here, at last, is the music hall tragedienne whose unexpected moderation and splendor—in a setting to match—will once more enchant the followers of her evolving career.

"But," repeats Josephine, "my inner battles are never-ending"—despite, we may add, her having refined all her gifts at this point. And she deplores the mechanical nature of extravagant, long-running revues.

* * *

In 1937, Josephine Baker became Madame Jean Lion.

In 1947, she became Madame Jo Bouillon.

Having not seen her country of birth for twelve years, she and Jo Bouillon soon left for the United States. But—alas!—on their own soil, Americans were unlike what they claimed to be when elsewhere. The French lieutenant Josephine Baker, decorated with the Médaille de la Résistance; the Black Venus, the only match for whose beauty were devotion and goodness itself, was obliged to travel in a special train carriage—and not with the whites, which was forbidden . . . At the Waldorf Astoria in New York, she was refused a room. No rooms there for colored citizens.

We understand that Josephine chose France as one chooses freedom; we may rejoice or despair over that. But the bighearted star held no grudge. Despite everything, she wanted to forget all pains, all prejudices, all that was not joie de vivre, a song or a dance.

"Do you remember what I wrote in *Le Tumulte Noir,* Paul Colin's portfolio? Let's go back to that . . ."

When the rage was in New York for colored people, Monsieur Ziegfeld of Ziegfeld Follies said it's getting darker and darker on old Broadway.

Since the "La Revue Nagri" came to Gay Parée,
I'll say it's getting darker and darker in Paris.

In a little while it shall be so dark until one shall light a match, then light another to see if the first ones lit are no longer.

As the old saying goes, I may be a dark horse but you will never be a black mare.

By the way, we can't forget the "Charleston," that mad dance. A friend asked me to pay them a visit.

But when I went to their house, people were in front of the house, and dogs were barking. I didn't know what to think, but in the end I decided to enter. Upon entering, the cat was hanging on the chandelier, the bird's cage turned over, dishes were broken, and the two people looked as if a terrible storm had happened. Of course with this sight, I didn't know what to do, go in or out. But being so curious I entered.

When they saw me, both stopped. The wife saying, which is right, Josephine? This way or that?

Then the husband said, no it isn't, I tell you this is the right way, isn't it Josephine?

As a matter of fact I didn't know what to say, so I asked if they would try to cool down a bit. I would try to see. All this time I didn't know what they were talking about.

When they stopped, they told me they were dancing the Charleston, and to make peace in the family I said both were right.[7]

We were now in the first days of March 1949, and I was waiting for Joséphine de Beauharnais in her dressing room.

This is who she was playing: Napoleon's first wife, in *Féeries et Folies,* the revue—rather, the musical—showing at the Folies Bergère. It was an audacious and charming venture by Messieurs Paul Derval and Michel Gyarmathy.

In this extravaganza, Josephine also played Mary, Queen of Scots. Queen of the spectacle . . .

Jean Barreyre, the most experienced of our theater critics, wrote:

> *She is an empress. A princess of the pose, with the elegance of a hummingbird; a voice that makes your heart sing. She is beautiful; fittingly, she dominates the ensemble with her great height and a talent that beams with kindness. She thanks the audience during the applause, and her joyous, silver-lined eyes seem to be brimming with sweet tears . . . This is the image of an unrivaled star of the music hall, endowed with all the attributes of this tremendous role.*[8]

"What do you say to carrying on with these memoirs, José?"

"Okay, but I only want to talk about fun things, even my memories of the war. You know, there were so many funny moments as well as the horrible ones . . . Ah! Would that be all right?"

Allow me to introduce Madame Lyne de Souza, another queen, the one who cut off my head in this particular scenario but who I liked all the same.

Josephine, hospitable and so unassuming, loves everyone she works with. There is not one of her colleagues, young or old, for whom she will not be a trusted, attentive friend and often a form of salvation. However, the moment we began to discuss her generosity, she stopped short. In an attempt to keep her charitable work afloat at the end of the war, she had become indebted by tens of millions of francs and resorted to pawning off her jewelry. "That's my business," she said. "It was my duty . . . Are you writing today? Good. Get yourself a seat . . . Madame, if you wouldn't mind . . . Well! To start with, that day I fell into the sea."

_____

I must apologize, for memoirs composed in this way cannot present the same appearance as a coherently unfolding narrative. This book ultimately presents itself in the form of reportage, a succession of interviews taking place at random intervals over more than twenty years. They simply form a collection of defining moments, impressions, and images, but in so doing, they give the most precise portrayal of the star that Paris has consecrated: once frenetic, now almost majestic, but always just as deeply moving.

1

FROM THE BANKS OF THE MISSISSIPPI TO THE BANKS OF THE SEINE

Childhood and Beginnings

St. Louis is a big city, a cold one, and it has a population of 800,000 . . . Working men and women, lots of Negroes, it's the city of 100,000 Negroes. The Mississippi is always full of yellow mud and it runs right through the middle, hidden under paddleboats and the black smoke rising from the flatboats taking cotton toward the ocean. Compared to the Mississippi, the Seine is just a little boy. There's an enormous multi-story bridge above the Mississippi. And St. Louis is full of railways, full of factories that give off their smoke above all the houses, and it is cold.

They sell everything: wood, grain, all sorts of flour, engines, cotton, corn . . .

St. Louis was founded by the French, you know, you can read about it. I was born there, on Bernard Street, June 3, 1906, state of Missouri, the United States of America, very beautiful and funny, *beau et très amusant.*

Write that they used to sell furs in St. Louis a long time ago, too.

My family was: a great-grandmother, a grandmother, my mother, my brother, and my two sisters. My father wasn't there, he was working far away.

My father and mother got to know each other at school. After, when they wanted to marry, their families didn't want them to. They got married anyway, but they were poor because nobody helped them. They were effectively abandoned. Then they decided to separate, so they could each work and provide for themselves. My mother lived with my grandmother, who was very poor, I remember that well; when I was a little girl, we were all terribly poor.

Then my great-grandmother died, and my grandmother, too. My father and my two sisters were working. Me, even more so. Now you understand, dear . . . I was the big man of the house.

I started school when I was five. I never stayed at one for long, though, because I used to fight with all the schoolmistresses and all the students. I didn't like being forced to do this, do that. I always preferred to be free. What's more, they wouldn't let me make funny faces. But our faces aren't made to sleep. Why don't we make more funny faces? What are we scared of? Making faces is a sport. A sport, just as important and interesting as the others!

But despite all the fights, and because of being punished so often and having to change school more than once, I became a good student, because I was interested in learning. I started to behave myself, and I learned.

I adored learning history; it still fascinates me. I'd like to know everything that people of all colors have done since the beginning of time. You can see their clothes change from one page to the next. That's what I like most about books.

At that time, I adored kings and queens above all else. I dreamed about them every night. I wanted to see kings and queens in real life. Sometimes I'd cry because I, too, wanted to be a queen. In my dreams, kings used to walk around with pointed shoes. They wore golden coats as long as roads, and the queens were blonde and walked down grand staircases. But the stairs were never-ending, so the kings and queens never reached me.

I also learned that there had been nasty kings. I was really surprised at first. To be a king and nasty, too, that simply shouldn't be! I would have liked to kill all the mean kings. Later, I promised myself that when I was strong I would fight everyone who was mean to the poor, whether they were kings or not.

Why did I become a dancer? Because I was born in a cold city, because I was very cold throughout my entire childhood, because I always wanted to dance in the theater.

In St. Louis, at my mother's, I had set up a little theater in the cellar. I wasn't yet ten years old. The curtain was made of pieces of cloth all joined together. And I put candles on top of cans of New Zealand peaches. The old candle stubs would light the way down the staircase—all three steps of it. The audience consisted of a dozen girls and boys, sat here and there on crates and an old bench.

I was the performer—I'd taken my mother's high heels and a dress so big I just disappeared inside it. I looked like a prisoner in a sack, or in one of those suits for deep-sea divers.

To enter my theater, you had to pay . . . one pin.

There was a performance every night.

And then the candles set fire to my dress. The audience ran away. I was alone in the cellar, with the fire. I managed to get the dress off in time. Just.

◆　◆　◆

I have always loved animals. Cats, dogs, monkeys, parrots, baby cows, goats. All animals, even snakes. I used to bring home all the abandoned or lost animals I met. My mother liked them, too, but then there were too many, and she didn't want them around. She threw them all out. And I followed them out: since my mother didn't want any more dogs and cats in the bedroom, I very often slept in the cellar with my dogs and my cats, after having a tea party with them. But I don't like rats, they're hypocrites. I know how they are, all born with tails like raw skin. I've seen how they creep up on everyone, how they stop, listen, run off, come back again.

I left school when I was eight years old to go and work.

We were all so very hungry and cold at home, Mama the only one making a little money . . . We couldn't go on like that.

Eight years old . . . It must have been 1914.

My aunt was the one who knew lots of people, and she wasn't as unhappy as Mama, so she set me up with work. It was always in the homes of American ladies, to look after their little children. Oh yes, I was happy! They're sweet and warm, little white children, and so delicate.

Another time, I was looking after little dogs, running errands, and helping in the kitchen. I was happy there, too. I loved those animals with all my heart.

At that point in my life, something terrible happened. I never talk about it to anyone, it hurts too much.

Listen, Monsieur Sauvage.

At the American lady's house where I looked after the little dogs, ran errands, and helped with the housework, one day they brought a chicken home. A little, live chicken, all white, kept in a wooden cage under the service table. We were friends, that chicken and I, and I named him Jacki. He had one little, round, golden eye that seemed to be mocking me, but I think he loved me all the same. That lasted some weeks. I looked after Jacki so well that he became a beautiful boy of a chicken with a delightful pink comb, and he started making lots of noise in the morning.

So, one day, the lady came into the kitchen, weighed up Jacki, and ordered me to kill him.

Do you know how chickens are killed—whether or not it's a chicken you love? You put it upside down between your legs and bam, you stab it in the throat. And it screams. It thrashes about. The blood spurts and gushes everywhere. Then the thrashing gets weaker and weaker, but you still need to hold on to it.

Oh! That memory . . . It taints my childhood.

Because no matter how hard I, too, tried to fight, and kiss Jacki, and beg, and refuse, and cry, the heartless American lady threatened to dismiss me on the spot, without paying me. At home, there was Mama, and the three kids, and my grandmother. And my aunt, who was a handful.

So there you have it, I did it, when I was all alone in the kitchen . . . I killed Jacki. I looked away and didn't once look back while he wriggled and writhed in between my legs. I tried to hold my breath so I wouldn't smell his poor blood. It was hot, almost black, as it dribbled into the bowl afterward, drip by drip.

But then I left, immediately after. I ran away . . . It was as if I'd been able to feel the very life of that little chicken fighting and squirming in the palms of my hands.

I went home. And since I hadn't brought back any money and never wanted to go back to that house again, or to any other, I'm sure I got a good beating . . .

I currently own seven dogs, three cats, a monkey, a parrot, two budgies, three white mice, a goldfish, and a snake who lies on the ground like a signature. I find animals interesting, and I like them because they're simple and complicated like little children.

Don't you find they move more beautifully than we do?

I had a little pig called Albert. My butler was called Albert, too, Albert Tartaglia, a nice man who worked hard. He certainly earned good money while working with me. He even bought himself a car, which I tried out, but I still can't drive very well.

Just look at him, my pig Albert! He would walk in such a funny way, to one side, wiggling his bottom, flapping his ears around like pieces of ribbon.

Cats love human sweat; sweat gets them excited—have you ever noticed? They'll rip up used underwear and eat it.

I also like the different poses my dolls can make; they have no bones . . . To the side like this, in front or behind like this, little drunk dolls in colorful rags.

Dolls and animals are the sort of company I prefer.

Every Sunday, I would go to watch dance shows for fifteen cents at the Booker T. Washington Theatre, a tiny theater with a tiny stage. There were just two boxes there, two squares with heads in them and rough patches of light on the performers' faces. I watched the different types of dances carefully, but I never liked the ballets. I've never liked dancers who use pointe work, either. They're like silly little birds, pip, pip, pip. It's madness! And with their wispy little dresses, too.

My childhood was the type where you have no stockings. I was cold, and I danced to keep warm.

I forgot to tell you about one of my first funny habits: I used to dress up as other people to see what would happen.

I would dress up in all sorts of ways, and I still do.

I would wander around, ringing on doorbells, asking for anything, and I would be happy when I met someone friendly. Then I'd run away . . .

When I was ten, I also went on my first trip. I went all the way to Philadelphia with my grandmother.

Grandma was a big colored lady who wore dresses with trains and big flowers and gigot sleeves, and on top, a big hat with a little hole in the middle, but my grandmother's bun could never fit in that little hole. I felt very proud to be out with my grandmother when she had that hat on. It was such a cheerful sight that everyone would turn around and laugh. Those days, generally on Sundays to go to Mass, they'd dress me in a pretty, white embroidered petticoat and make sure it stuck out so people could see it . . . But we only had the one petticoat, of course, for three daughters. So we wore it in turns, over many years, and Mama was very sad that she could never take the three of us out together.

I went barefoot most of the time. That's how I met with an old nail; it went into my heel. Oh my, Monsieur Sauvage, how it hurt! I hadn't told anyone, but then it got infected. So they took me to the hospital one evening. The man spent a few days deciding what to do. He said they might have to cut off my foot.

After that episode, I was sent back to school, to stop me from loitering in the streets. But on Thursdays and Sundays I still played dress-up, naturally.

And, naturally, one day I dressed up as "my grandmother" but with false red hair. I wore her dress with a train and took her white parasol. But the hat. Oh, what a hat! Oh, goodness, I need to laugh for a minute.

While I was still going to school, I played, or rather, I *appeared*, in the theater, on Mondays and Fridays every week, supervised by my aunt, another big lady and a handful, too.

I didn't have time to rehearse but I did my best. I lost myself in the music.

I would always say I was older than I was. That's how I came to earn nine dollars a week. But most of the time I got nothing because the revue didn't do well.

Then I was finally sixteen. I developed very quickly. I was just as tall and strong at sixteen as I am now, with a little less bosom.

Always healthy.

So, when I turned sixteen, I thought long and hard, thought some more, and then:

1. I cut my hair.
2. I left my family.

"You can't do anything," I thought, "with your family on your back."

I love colors for what they are, blood red, blinding yellow, egg yolk . . . Colors have an amazing physical effect on me: they intoxicate me, thrill me. I used to go nearly every day to visit the repair works they were doing at Les Acacias, the tearoom near Place de l'Étoile, where I'd dance in the afternoons. And do you know what I would do? I would play with the paint cans, and by the end my head hurt as if I'd drunk too much!

Paint is full of alcohol.

Gold powder is a wondrous thing. I would take a big handful, rub my arms in it, and smear it on my face. I'd have gladly taken a shower in it: a shower of gold dust.

I made my debut in Philadelphia—the city of bookstores and editors—in the Standard Theatre, a small theater, in a dreadful revue. I made ten dollars a week.

But really, I made nothing at all because they almost never

paid, and I was always hungry. I was empty, empty enough to snap in two. My teeth were falling out. I was thinking about New York, about big money, about life in a treasure of a coat.

One fine day, I left for New York. All I had was my ticket. I was in the last car, standing on the platform. From there, the rails joined into a point as far out as I could see.

New York is men versus women.

I went straight to a music hall on Broadway.

At the Broadway music hall, 63rd Street, the director said, "Come back tomorrow."

He said that every day for a week, and I had nothing left to eat.

I didn't know where to sleep, I spent three days without food, I was sleeping in a park. The ground sweated at night; a cold fever. I'd get up and run. Shadows would run behind me, dancing like I would never be able to. But still, I slept, exhausted, on grass, on leaves, under branches.

I went back again to see the director.

"No, no, no!" he shouted. "You're too young, you're just a kid, we can't. Plus, you're ugly. Ugly body, ugly face. Goodbye!"

But I just wanted to work, I wanted to dance. So I went back again to see the director. I stood outside the door for more than an hour and I wanted to cry. At last, I knocked. I went inside. The director saw me.

"Well, fine!" he said. "Since you're insisting, you'll join the second company and go on tour."

We traveled from one town to the next for six months. In the smaller towns, we played in covered schoolyards.

The boys flirted with me but the other girls did not like me.

"You act and sing like a monkey!" they would shout in my face.

"That's how I dance and that's how I always will dance. Soon enough, I'll be the one giving work to all of *you*." That's what I told them.

They were horrible, but the manager was even worse. When we were traveling, he made sure everyone had a room for the night except me. And he never put my name on the programs.

Eventually, the entire company came back to Brooklyn.

One night, the top director at 63rd Street saw me performing in the revue. After staring at me for a long while, he came to speak to me:

"Come to my place tomorrow, it's important."

I was there the next day, of course.

"I'll give you twenty dollars a week to perform here. Come with me!"

Backstage, he showed me a corner where I could get dressed and do my makeup. It was an awful place. I had to sit on the ground with my makeup box. It was cold there, too. Water trickled onto my shoulders, drop by drop. Naturally, I fell ill. I stayed in bed for a week and then—since I needed to survive—I went back to the theater. But first, I telephoned my mother: "Mama, things are looking up."

My mother was ill at the time. She got better.

Shuffle Along was the first major colored show in New York, a three-act musical. We performed it for two years nonstop, 1923 and 1924, in the same theater, 63rd Street Music Hall. The producers: Miller and Lyles, Sissle and Blake.

Then I left *Shuffle Along*.

But there really were some great artists there: Edith Spencer and Lottie Gee danced and sang very well.

And while I was there, I moved from the second row in the chorus to the first, because I went cross-eyed studying the music and could fling my arms and legs over the audience members' heads.

I was working to support my mother, my sisters, and my little brother, who lived in Washington.

One day, all the papers, the dailies and the weeklies, were talking about me.

"This is it," I thought.

Once the revue finished, I forgot about it. I forget all my roles, one after the other . . .

I danced in *Chocolate Dandies*, fists on my hips, knees together—and then I changed again.

In a nutshell, there I was at the Plantation Club, 42 Broadway. It's very nice, the Plantation, with good jazz: they really pull out all the stops.

Dick played the banjo with his big black mouth wide open so you could see his huge red tongue inside. He didn't eat me, though, Dick, not him or any of the others.

Before meeting Mrs. Reagan, I already wanted to go and perform in Europe.

Mrs. Reagan had seen me perform my tiny role in the second

company of that Broadway music hall. Then she had lost track of me, didn't know where to find me when she saw me by chance at the Plantation, where I was working.

I was very lucky: one night, the star of the show couldn't perform; I was allowed to take her place. The audience loved me more than her . . .

When she came back, this star, she was really mad at me. She tried hard to get me dismissed, but I stood firm and I stayed.

I was making one hundred and twenty-five dollars a week.

"Come and work for me," Mrs. Reagan said. "I'll give you one hundred and fifty dollars a week."

I accepted at first and then refused.

"I'll give you two hundred dollars!"

"Well, I'll think about it."

"Fine. I'll give you two hundred and fifty dollars."

So I accepted.

You know, Monsieur Sauvage, as far back as my memories go, I can only recall one day in my whole life when I felt frightened. A day that only lasted an hour, maybe a minute, when I struggled between a past full of sadness and my uncertain future, like a person drowning in the night, when the current is carrying them away and suddenly they've had enough . . . One minute when fear had such a tight hold on me, on my head, my heart, my stomach, that I could have broken apart.

September 15, 1925 . . .

The *Berengaria,* Captain W. R. D. Irvine—pulled by four little towboats that were straining like crazy at the ropes—was taking off slowly from the docks in New York. It was leaving the city. The sea was calm and all red in the setting sun. I was walking, and I was so anxious, along the walkway next to the sea. No one to take notice of me. And why would they? Who would have reached out to me, said a few words? I was just a little showgirl—not even that, a little black girl . . .

The Statue of Liberty disappeared beyond the sea. I was finished with America. I had to start again, perhaps begin from nothing . . . Would I be strong enough, ambitious enough? Europe . . . Paris . . .

It was only when the ship and the sea were covered in night's cloak that I felt the fear draining away. That I was alive, that I was free. That I was no longer dreadfully alone, but joyfully alone.

And to prove it was really over, I began to sing to myself, a sweet song, sweeter than the song of the salty water against the *Berengaria*'s iron sides:

I saw the splendor of the moonlight
On Honolulu Bay
There's something tender in the moonlight
On Honolulu Bay

Goodbye, New York . . . Goodbye, Philadelphia . . . Goodbye, St. Louis . . . Goodbye, little girl with the purple hands . . . Goodbye, rats at Bernard Street . . . Goodbye . . .

It was as if I'd suddenly woken up in the middle of the night. There were shadows.

I tiptoed forward. I chased the shadows and they disappeared, melting when they met the electric lights on the decks, in the cabins, and in the drawing rooms filled with peals of laughter and music.

The secret to holding on was not to move, to enjoy this wonderful show for myself, and only myself, for the first time.

I looked at the ship for another minute, lit up from top to bottom. I closed my eyes. A never-ending game, all these sad or funny shades; my dream in black and white.

A journey as smooth as oil.

I took part in the concerts organized on board, of course. Take a look at the program: "Brown Eyes" and "If You Hadn't Gone Away," by Miss Baker, performer. September 16 . . .

September 18. Everyone was on deck. Alert. Everyone was stepping into lifebelts, untying the lifeboats; the women were screaming. The sailors were calmly doing their jobs. We could hear the pulleys screeching, the little children, too. But the ocean was as quiet as ever. It was green and shiny.

So, what was the problem?

There was a mine drifting around somewhere nearby. Luckily, we didn't bump into it.

I've heard a lot about the Great War. What a thing to have happened.

I understand nothing about it, I admit, but it moves me to tears. It makes me feel awfully sorry. Men who only have one arm, one leg, or one eye: I suffer for them. I pity them with all my heart.

I hate anyone who hurts others. The unfortunate are all my

children, I would like them to all be my children. Just as waiters, cooks, and barmen are my brothers, and young maids are my sisters.

Cherbourg. It was cold. It had been too hot in New York. All I had was a little coat that was barely there. I caught a bad cold. In the port, there was our huge boat among lots of little ones. Around the city were tiny trams, small but so sweet, those little trams!

There was no time to lose. We ran from customs to the special train that was waiting for us, already letting off steam in the station. I didn't have French money; I gave twenty dollars to a porter.

"No, madame," he said. "No, I don't want it, not good."

So I gave him thirty, and he took it.

The same day, September 22, four hours later: Paris.

How lucky—it was raining! That was a good sign. If it's raining in a city where you find yourself for the first time, that's good luck.

Oh, it was so funny! Little houses, little streets, little sidewalks. "I'll never be able to dance here," I thought. "This is all too small. Where are New York's long, straight lines?"

And I didn't know French at all. And I'd only brought ridiculous little dresses like the ones young American girls wear with flat shoes.

In France, the houses are small, but women's heels are very high.

+ + +

Let me tell you what I wore when I went for my first walk around Paris.

My outfit made everybody laugh. Now I understand why everybody laughed, and I laugh about it more than all of them.

Imagine . . .

I wore a checked dress with pockets, held up by two checked straps that went over my checked blouse.

I had a feathered hat perched on my head. And to top it all, I had a camera hanging down by my left buttock and a huge pair of binoculars by my right. I've never known why but when Americans go to a foreign country, they must always have binoculars and a camera swinging behind them.

I wore bobby socks and flat heels.

Ah, I looked so pretty that day, to go and see the Arc de Triomphe and Napoleon's tomb!

2

PARIS NEWS AND VIEWS

I will always remember our first rehearsal for *La Revue Nègre* at the Théâtre des Champs-Élysées. They still didn't know about the Charleston. The room was dark, the stage was lit up. There were twenty people sitting in the first row.

Hello, Charleston! The stagehands were watching, the two fire officers were astounded. They weren't used to trombones hitting them in the stomach like that.

Furthest away, behind the flats, the youngest ones were trying to copy us. They wanted to dance the Charleston! When no one was looking, they were shaking their flanneled legs, they were kicking the air—and the co-worker next to them, too.

All the theater staff came to watch us secretly: the typists were looking through a hole in the backdrop, the two fire officers were laughing into their helmets, the twenty people in the front row were jiggling their legs . . . The Charleston had already got a hold of them; they had ants in their shoes.

Yes sir, that's my baby.

———

Europeans first saw the Charleston danced by Negroes. They invented another version that's hardly anything like the original, but it is very good. You're supposed to dance the Charleston wearing strings of shells that shake against your skin and make a dry sound. But I replaced the shells with bananas and feathers.

You've got to dance with your hips, one then the other, one foot over the other, sticking out your buttocks and waving your arms . . . We've been hiding our buttocks too much for too long. Buttocks exist. I don't know why we dislike them. There are also buttocks that are terribly silly, of course, terribly pretentious, terribly mediocre. All they are good for is sitting on, if that.

The French were immediately kind. Every sort of person took a liking to me, to us.

La Revue Nègre.

Poor Douglas, I danced with him.

He was extraordinary.

He's dead now.

He was like rubber.

I can still hear the soles of his shoes clicking in my ears.

Louis Douglas, he could imitate any sound in the world, a racehorse, a railway, clickety-clack, clickety-clack, clickety-clack, in front of a black backdrop with a little white church. His lips were white, too. He also had a pink collar, and he really did dance in silence. He's dead now, poor Doug . . .

Well, I thought he was dead, but he's alive. I heard he was spending time in Marseille. I'm so happy to hear that.

Doug should go back to America and put together a new Negro troupe! You still don't know everything that Negroes have to offer.

✦ ✦ ✦

Have we said enough about Paris's place in the world and life in Paris?

Paris is elegance, mayhem, love, champagne and pretty trinkets, the Eiffel Tower. Spirit and heart, wouldn't you say? And thousands of other things, thousands of other adjectives. I soon understood Paris, and I loved it passionately. To begin, Paris adopted me from the very first night. It celebrated me, gave me everything . . . Loved me, too, I hope. Paris is dance, and I love dance.

Pretty women, pretty dresses. The seasons would present them to us one after the other. Here he is: Spring, the latest addition, the child who will soon become Prince Summer!

Paris is women, sun, midnight sun. The Bois, tea, dance halls, shopping, cabaret.

A woman . . .

Is she the same one? I don't recognize her. This morning she was so ordinary, so covered up in a rather plain dress, and now here she is tonight, all flesh and pearls.

I love Paris, how it moves, how it sounds, its mystery—its mysteries—all its mysteries. I'm not simply parroting out the same old compliments, I'm trying to understand . . . to imagine . . .

Where could they go, all these women I come across? Busy women, relaxed women, smiling, worried. Is it work? An obsession with work and time ticking by? Meeting a lover? An important errand—the couturier, most likely? What a telltale I am, but yes, the couturier, then the lover, because she needs to look her best. But love can dress her better than any couturier.

A small woman with short hair, driving down a dusty, dirty road in a big car, eyes straight ahead, brow furrowed. But soon she'll be at the restaurant, her face relaxed, and how she will laugh! Dinners at the water's edge, the River Seine, the Marne and the Oise, or under the trees. Smiles, eyes filled with promise. Going home at night. Faint shadows, flashing headlights, lying in his arms for a while when it's cold.

Nighttime, champagne, joy, frenzy, more dancing, flowers, women.

Never horrid, never stupid, never ordinary . . . *Vive Paris!*

But I know that there are poor people, too, and I think about them . . .

I have moved house very often. I like all the quartiers in Paris.

I lived on Rue Henri-Rochefort, Avenue Pierre 1er de Serbie, Rue Fromentin, and others.

I lived in a palace on the Champs-Élysées. There was a swimming pool in the middle of the apartment, all in marble; it took two months to build. It cost a fortune, that swimming pool, but my favorite thing in that palace was my baby jaguar.

And I will never forget Rue Henry-Monnier in Montmartre where all the showgirls from the revue would sleep.

We would eat at La Poule au Pot for fifteen francs each, and I was happy, very happy.

Then I was sued, for the first time: Mrs. Dudley. She gave me one thousand dollars a month for *La Revue Nègre*. But I met some people; I left.

Mrs. Dudley was very fond of me, but that's not my fault. She wanted me to give her two hundred thousand francs. I know nothing about lawsuits—well, I don't *want* to know anything about them.

I was sued again, by a dance hall. They wanted me to give them three hundred thousand francs.

I was sued a third time. There was a big couturier involved. But his appeal was rejected: he was *débouté*, as they say here—that's funny . . . *débouté, dégoûté*. I'll have others, of course, other lawsuits. It just happens that way sometimes, you see? People try to push their luck.

Presents, pretty presents: a mountain of them and me.

I've been given rings with fire opals as big as eggs; I've been given a pair of very old earrings that belonged to a duchess one hundred and fifty years ago; I've been given pearls like teeth; flowers that came from Italy on the same day, in baskets filled with moss—I also wanted flowers that could eat flies and even meat, with long hairs and glue in the middle. I've been given six Chinese lacquer chairs. I've been given toys that ran on electricity; I've been given dirty bottles and a vase from the Netherlands; little ivory elephants from Russia, carved by poor people from the North Pole; a stuffed bear, a stuffed duck, a stuffed rabbit, a stuffed cat, and lots of other stuffed animals. I've been given live animals. A pair of golden shoes; a dress that stayed folded up in my red handbag. Enormous peaches. Another time, enormous strawberries. I've been given perfume in a glass horse. One fur, two furs, three furs, four furs, a whole army of animal skins. Bracelets with red stones for my arms, my wrists, my legs. I don't remember.

Quite enough.

Nowadays, all I want are little animals. I did treat myself to a ring, though, for eighty thousand francs; it was very nice. I don't know where that ring is now. It's probably over there in a little box. I don't like jewelry that much.

The last present during that time: Monsieur Donnet gave me a marvelous car. That thing was speedy. A sedan, special model, upholstered entirely in snakeskin. A snakeskin dream, a snakeskin feast, a wonder, a snakeskin wonder.

I got my driving license at Porte Maillot, June 7, 1927. "Go forward, stop, go forward, turn, adjust your speed . . . Very good, Mademoiselle, you've passed."

Later, I would get my pilot's license, behind Versailles, in 1936.

But I'm not very sporty, I don't exercise. Only very little. That's how I live, randomly. I don't rehearse, like a machine. I'm not a machine. And randomness is more beautiful than a machine, I know that.

Josephine Baker, voilà!

I turn my shoulder like it's a cog in my machine-body. I play marbles with my eyes. I stretch out my lips when I please. I walk on my heels when I please. I race around on all fours when I please. I brush off any stares. After all, I'm not a pin cushion. I tell you who I am with my hands, my arms. I row through the air, I swim through the air. I sweat, I jump, and voilà!

Dear Monsieur Marcel Sauvage,

You will certainly be quite surprised at receiving this letter. I would like to apologize immediately for the liberty that I have taken in writing to you. I ask you not to hold this against me.

I have learned, through reading Les Nouvelles Littéraires, *that you are endeavoring to write Josephine Baker's memoirs. While I know nothing about this project nor the manner in which you intend to lead this venture, I would like to congratulate you for undertaking such fascinating work, and I pray wholeheartedly for its success.*

The reason I write to you is that I knew Josephine Baker very well. I will not trouble you with the full story of this affair. You must understand that it has never been possible for me to ascertain whether I held a place in the life of this extraordinary woman— especially since I cannot speak English. However, I believe that if she were to tell you about her life in detail, in particular her arrival in Paris, then she would certainly relate to you the beginnings of her success and perhaps she would tell you about a passionate spectator who would attend her shows regularly, sit in the same seat, and applaud until his hands bled. This character, I admit, was rather too impassioned. You might have guessed that I was this captivated audience member. You will understand why

I feel driven to write to you when I tell you that I wish to bury my past as a spectator of Josephine Baker for good.

Perhaps you will smile. Perhaps Josephine Baker has not mentioned any of this to you. If this is the case, please consider this letter rescinded and accept my apologies for having written it. If, on the contrary, Josephine Baker has told you this story, I kindly ask you to inform me but not to inform the public. In either situation, I ask you not to discuss this letter with Miss Baker, to excuse my approach, and, please, to send a reply.

With my highest and most sincere regards.

Oh, là là! Put that paper away, there are plenty more of that type.

Admirers are a race of their own, an odd race. They all write in the same way. They all sign their letters with "A. B. C. D. E. F. G. . . . or Y. Z., your admirer." They all have odd ideas, an odd physique, an odd style, an odd hat, an odd way of looking at you . . . Half of them don't even have a fixed address.

I knew one who would lock himself in the Théâtre des Champs-Élysées after the show so he could "admire" me again the next evening. He couldn't afford another ticket. He'd spend all night and all day under the rows of seats. He'd eat bars of chocolate.

It's very important to believe in God. I believe there is no better source of strength. Say what you will. Every evening I say a prayer, a prayer that I think up myself and that I sing to the tune of a song. Once before going onstage and once more before going to sleep. And always, wherever I am and no matter how tired I may be, I pray. I have been let down so many times, but I'm not bitter. I have loved many times. But that's my business.

One night at the Folies Bergère, one of the first nights, I was in my dressing room completely naked. I was feeling sad, because there are certain sad things that I keep for my prayers. I was on my knees, hands clasped, head bowed. The stage manager stormed in without knocking. I don't like being disturbed. I looked at the fellow in such a way that he left quietly and closed the door quietly behind him. And I finished my prayer.

I danced at Monsieur Dreyfus's house. I danced for everyone and I sang when I was invited to.

I danced on the famous Pont d'Argent, the Silver Bridge, at the Bal des Petits Lits Blancs charity gala for the little children at the Opéra, where they lit forty thousand gold lamps.

White and gold, white and silver, chandeliers, garlands, drapes, and right beneath the bridge, hands everywhere, waving above upturned faces.

It was as if I was singing above all of Paris, crowded, crowded with tailcoats. Monsieur Poincaré was in a very small box, with his small gray beard. I tossed my leg up into his eyeline from afar. He laughed.

At Christmas time in 1926, I paid for a Christmas tree in the theater, for the children of the policemen of Paris. A fir tree, tiny candles, glass eggs, biscuits, toys . . .

I had been dreaming of this for a long time. To be a Mother Christmas, a young colored Mother Christmas. I was more over-joyed that day than all the little ones, I'm sure I was, more de-lighted than any of them, as happy as a little girl. The applause that came from those little hands is still my greatest achievement.

But I was furious when I noticed that there were many children there whom I hadn't invited, among the ones that I had. Little children from rich families who didn't care about my presents, who'd come in their patent shoes with their parents. Snobs. I will never forgive the ones who were responsible for that. Next time, here's what I'll do: I will buy sweets and toys myself, and I will go to the hospitals myself to give them to the unfortunate children there, with their poor little sad faces.

These things help me forget my own childhood and the snow that falls on St. Louis and the Negroes in their cold houses and the house on Bernard Street where we were so poor.

✦ ✦ ✦

Now I have what I want: a huge dictionary, in seven volumes, full of pictures. No, I don't look inside it, I don't have the time. I weigh up each volume, and it makes me laugh. Everything makes me laugh. It's not my fault. But words aren't that heavy.

Why?

I'm reading something right now. Here it is: *Contes Dorés*. Yes, fairy tales, the loveliest books.

Here's a story you might not know: the one about the man who loved insects.

All his life, he walked on his hands with his legs in the air so he wouldn't squash the little creatures and so he could see the smallest ones better: gold, silver, shiny, all the ones you can think of . . . little barrels raised up on needles, one behind the other, and ready to sting.

Now I'm going to reveal my secret. I must tell you the story of the rabbit's foot.

In short, I've been lucky, very lucky throughout my life. You should take pity on the girls you see dancing in the music hall, behind the footlights. What happens to them when the curtain falls? One in a thousand, in a million maybe, becomes a star. The others burn out before their time.

I know it, and I owe everything to my rabbit's foot.

I was still performing at 64th Street when, one evening, I caught sight of a little man waiting for me at my dressing room door.[9] He was a strange-looking man, with hair as ginger as a carrot, eyes popping out of his head, and a droopy shoulder.

"Here," he said right away. "I've come from South Carolina, where I met a family friend of yours. He gave me this gift to give to you. Keep it safe, it'll bring you good luck. It's a rabbit's foot."

I hadn't been very happy around that time and had often—as one should—looked over my left shoulder at the new moon while shaking a coin in the palm of my right hand. But I still hadn't become rich . . .

So I took the rabbit's foot.

The next day, at the same time, I found the same ginger-haired man at the door of my dressing room. "You must never lose that rabbit's foot," he said. "It's your greatest treasure, miss. If you lose it, I swear, you'll end up with no job at all. Goodbye!"

He clicked his tongue and disappeared backstage among all the scenery.

I put the rabbit's foot in my powder box.

That night, I slept with it under my pillow.

The next day, at the same time, I thought that perhaps the little man would be there again. But this time there was a tall, thin man at my dressing room door. "You must be Mademoiselle Baker."

He handed me an envelope. In it was a letter that read, "Come and see me for a job."

I ran. I couldn't breathe. I arrived. I knocked.

"Come in . . . Would you like to dance at the new Plantation Club, on Broadway? Here's your contract."

I left. I laughed. I danced. I was so glad about my rabbit's foot. Out on the street, I kissed it, kissed it for an hour.

Six months later, I had a job in Paris.

✦　✦　✦

One day, at the Théâtre des Champs-Élysées, I couldn't find my rabbit's foot.

I was desperate. I looked absolutely everywhere. I scoured backstage, my bedroom, the hotel—nothing.

However, there was another showgirl in the troupe, Josie Smith, who, soon after I lost it, had signed a contract with the director of a music hall in London. I had my suspicions.

I went into Josie's dressing room one day—and there she was, this Josie, using my rabbit's foot as a puff for her rice powder. Ah! Just what I had feared! We had a fight, but that night I slept soundly with my dear rabbit's foot under my bolster cushion.

A few days later I was at the races, at Longchamp. It was the Prix de l'Arc de Triomphe. "Let's place a bet," I thought, "since you have your rabbit's foot." I bet on two horses; I won four hundred thousand francs.

That is my secret: a rabbit's foot.

Josephine Baker often says: "The things I enjoy are the end of me."

That is her motto.

And she makes use of it. The following two stories will be your proof.

It is time for Josephine to take to the stage. The theater is full. Everyone is waiting, opera glasses at the ready. But the star is nowhere to be seen. The search begins: she is not in the stairwell, not in her dressing room, not in the theater at all. The stage manager howls, rings all the bells. He pulls at his hair—rather, he would if he had any. He sends a car to Josephine's home. Nobody.

At the theater, the running order is reversed. The orchestra plays an additional march. In short, it is a disaster. The director is white as a sheet, so to speak.

Josephine is, in fact, with the concierge. It so happens that she had arrived early that day.

"What a wonderful soup!" she had said, picking up the aroma from the concierge's dressing room.

Josephine asked if she could taste the soup. She ended up eating it all, with a Camembert for good measure. A few bottles of champagne were sent for.

"What's happening here? Unbelievable!"

Josephine rushes off, climbs the stairs four at a time, undresses and puts on her skimpy red costume.

And now here she is, onstage, her arms borne upward by the applause.

"What delicious soup!"

Another day, at the same time, there is no one with the concierge, no one in the stairwell, no one. Josephine is no longer backstage. There is no answer to the knocking on her dressing room door. It is locked. Cue pandemonium, rushing about, more music . . .

Eventually, the anxious director has the door opened. There is Josephine. She is reclining naked on the floor with a langouste and a pair of scissors. She is cutting up the langouste and thoroughly enjoying herself.

Josephine leaps to her feet. When she takes to the stage, she is still chewing her last mouthful of langouste. A superb langouste.

N.B.—Josephine Baker is now keeping rabbits in her dressing room. The theater director complains about the rabbit droppings and the foul smell.

3

FIRST TOUR OF
THE OLD AND NEW WORLDS

n just over two years, from 1928 to 1930, I visited twenty-five
countries in Europe and America.

The Netherlands

We went slowly over a big bridge—it must have been several kilometers long, at least that's what I thought—a big bridge over yellow, sleepy water with no reflection, a flat surface of water and
sludge. Suddenly, at the end of the bridge, there was the Netherlands.

The canals in the fields are like roads, but you can't see them.
You'd have thought the vehicles had wings—sailboats in no hurry.

The great theater in Rotterdam.

The Scala Theatre in the Hague.

The Palais de Danse in Scheveningen.

The Concertgebouw in Amsterdam.

What I like about success, Monsieur Sauvage, is the love that goes into it and not so much the surprise or the wonder, and certainly not the admiration. So, being a curiosity was a very tough job for me. Yes, what a thankless job. I can show you the contracts from my European tour: each time, after the theater and music hall shows, I had to go and dance in the cabarets, doing my own special numbers and entertaining people like I did in my cabaret in Montmartre. It was written in the contracts: "Entertain people" . . . Tweaking the beards of good old gentlemen, flattering the fat ladies, making them dance in their fancy coats and stiff outfits, you know the sort of thing. People really need their fun these days. And they thought I was having fun, too, naturally. Sometimes I did, but not in the way you might think. This all started in 1928, with the Netherlands.

It was in the Tuschinski cabaret, a great place, and they gave me a warm welcome. But what I love is when people love me, that's all.

Dutch people are serious and rosy. They eat well and don't smile often, but when they do, they really mean it. Nearly all of them are strong, like the seawalls in their country. Everyone can speak three or four languages without a fuss.

I soon became known around the Netherlands.

Once, in a small, clean town—and quiet, so quiet—some people stopped me in the street. They tugged at my sleeve and asked me to dance. So I danced. Everyone was happy. There was a woman watching me with a small child in her arms, a pretty baby, and I picked him up. I wanted to kiss him, rock him a little; I would have liked to have danced with him a little, too, but his mother gave me a dirty look, and before I knew it, she'd snatched him away . . . Do you understand? She took her child away from the savage.

People think I've come straight out of the wilderness. I believe that in certain areas of the Netherlands—and the other countries I visited—people would have happily fed me ground glass. Primitive instincts, of course, folly of the flesh, chaos of the senses, frenzied animality—was this all they could say? White imagination is something else when it comes to colored folk. And the prejudices are the same everywhere.

But now Paris is my wilderness. I love it with all my heart, and that love is like wine—that I can't drink because it goes straight to my little head. I can't drink at all. But Paris gets me drunk. You know, I worked wholeheartedly for two years abroad so I could come back to Paris and so that Paris, when I came back, could applaud me as I hoped to deserve it.

Forgive me . . . We were in the Netherlands.

There we were in the countryside. Nothing but little, low houses with lots of flowers, and the women of these houses going about their business among the geese. It was so pretty . . .

"Money, money!" Children would run in groups behind my manager, Pepito, and me, shouting with their lovely red, puffy cheeks, "Money, money!"

Honestly, what a strange fish! How rich she must be! So, to make those lovely cheeks and blue eyes happy, we gave them little coins, clean and shiny like all the tiles in the Netherlands.

The Hague is the capital of bicycles and red bricks. The policemen have big white gloves like Negro comedians wear in revues.

Rotterdam and Amsterdam: there's a lot more happening, they're livelier; boats, trade, and they're full of color, patches and fragments of every color like pieces of glass in those telescopes you twist around, you know?

The Dutch like big colors, real colors, like red and yellow.

I spent one month in that country of water, sand, and fir trees. August to September 1928. And I learned to love it. I'd like to love all countries. To do that, you must also dress like they do in that country. So I dressed like a Dutch lady, with a white bonnet; a big, long, voluminous dress; and yellow clogs. Yes, I danced the Charleston in yellow clogs! And I carried milk in big iron churns. We laughed, Pepito most of all; he laughed like crazy. I don't smoke, ever; otherwise I would have smoked a clay pipe like the fishermen's wives and the fishermen themselves and the villagers in their wide trousers and fur hats.

In Scheveningen, the women wear gold antennas on top of their bonnets, just above their foreheads, that shake when they walk. It makes them look like insects. Tall women in black cloaks. Beautiful women. And the sea in Scheveningen is almost always gloomy and wrinkled, pulling ugly faces. The sea doesn't have a classic face there; it isn't always shiny. But there is such a magnificent avenue between the trees, with promenades taking you from the Hague to Scheveningen, to Scheveningen Beach, where the brass players shine.

I'm not talking about my performances. I think they were a

hit, since they asked me to come back to the Netherlands one day . . .

Beautiful cheeses, tulips, and chocolate; it's marvelous.

"Kiss my nose, Monsieur Sauvage, and please . . . don't be upset with me anymore . . ."

"It's not my fault," continues Josephine, tilting her head over her "machine-shoulder," "if, in my memory, there are no borders between the countries I've performed in. I don't like the borders that people create; I don't pay much attention to them. First of all, right now it is today. Why spoil it with yesterday? You want me to? Well, all right . . . How about Denmark, Sweden, and Norway?"

Denmark, Sweden, and Norway

They are the three politest countries.

I like politeness.

You know, once in Central Europe—or maybe it wasn't Europe at all—one evening, directly ahead of me in the front row, I saw a man reading a big, open newspaper while I was singing. The next day, in the same seat: the same man, with his open newspaper again—hiding his disgust behind it, I suppose. On the third day, I first looked through the hole in the curtain—and the newspaper was there. So, I made my entrance on tiptoes, went all the way to the orchestra, bent down ever so slowly toward the conductor, and I motioned to him to stop the music.

"Can't you see, Mr. Conductor," I called, "that this gentleman has been trying to read his newspaper for three days?"

Then I said to the man, who had finally put his newspaper down: "Excuse me, sir, but I understood perfectly well the first time. Now, do you mind?"

Copenhagen, Oslo, Stockholm, and Gothenburg: forty-five days, from the month of June to the month of August 1928.

Copenhagen: "Following the performance at the Dagmar Theater, to sing, dance, and entertain the clients at the Adlon club, in the same manner as at her cabaret on Rue Fontaine in Paris."

Stockholm: "Following the performance at the Oscar Theater, to sing, dance, and entertain the clients in the Winter Garden at the Grand Hôtel, in the same manner as . . ."

Oslo: "Following the performance . . . to sing, dance, and entertain the clients . . ."

That way, everyone is happy.

They are the cleanest countries I know, and the politest. So polite, it scared me at first. But it's crazy just how clean everything is in those countries, Monsieur Sauvage. It's wonderful: you can lean against anything you like. What's more—and it's true, I swear to you, I wouldn't say it if it wasn't—I was very successful there. You'll see for yourself.

In Copenhagen, I danced for a royal family for the first time, to great applause.

In Stockholm, I performed for the king himself. But if you ask what he was like, I couldn't tell you. When I dance, I dance. I don't look at anyone, not even the king.

There were so, so many people packed outside my hotel in Copenhagen, waiting under my window. It was nice weather that day. I had the not-so-clever idea to throw some photographs down . . . and with what happened next—I have never seen so many squashed straw hats. Those poor hats made me want to laugh, but deep down I was very touched.

Every evening in Oslo, two handsome policemen on horseback would accompany me from the exit of the theater to my hotel. It was nice. But they're always embarrassing, policemen, especially on horseback, and I was a little worried. People would look at us. And so I would make little jokes to the policemen, to show people I hadn't been arrested. Casually, you see?

In Stockholm, I had six policemen on foot to protect me from curious people. They saluted me like I was a general. I had to crane my neck to look at them. They were enormous, those policemen. I was so small in Sweden.

The sun is a comedian over there. It rains, then all of a sudden it's sunny again. Then it rains, then . . . oh, là là!

The midnight sun is really something else. You go into the theater and it's light. You leave the theater and it's still light, but it's night.

I went fishing under the midnight sun. The air was pure, the boat was rocking, turning, swaying at the whim of the sails and the fjord's bends. We could see everything clearly outlined in the cold light. But then a terrible little breeze came, strong and sharp like a blade of ice.

What a to-do, Monsieur Sauvage. They set me up under the sunshade that covered the table. It smelled like lard, fish, old leather, tar, and sailors' sorrows. I felt sick. And yet it was the sea itself that calmed me. I could hear it beating regularly against the boat's hull, against the front of the hull, trying to break the little mast that was sticking out, you know? But it soothed me, despite everything. It sent me to sleep. Oh, and I tell you what, the water I thought was outside was actually inside. Yes, it was hitting the boat from the outside, but then it got in and sloshed around.

I will always remember fishing in the fjords . . .

In Copenhagen, every house has a mast, like on a boat, and every Sunday, they hoist a flag up on every mast. How lovely, and funny, don't you think?

Stockholm is a city of banners, surrounded by water and islands. I saw Einar Lundborg there, in the theater, the aviator who had just rescued General Nobile. He came to my dressing room to say hello. I didn't know what to say. What could I, a colored dancer, say to a hero? When I meet someone I admire, I just stay quiet. But it made me so, so happy. He was humble and seemed so sweet, that man. The only person with him was his wife, on his arm. And the King of Sweden was there with the entire royal family.

But I didn't conquer Stockholm as easily as it may seem. Stockholm is a high-class city full of wary people. They were wary of my banana belt—which I know very well wasn't a life preserver, since, as you say, they tried to sink me with it. Anyway, the news-papers got a debate going, but one journalist, Monsieur Berman, defended me so graciously. "How many whites here have a black heart?" he wrote. "This is about an art form that is new to us, not about a naked woman. In any case, this woman has never been naked before her audience. Will Stockholm really refuse to wel-come someone who has conquered Paris?" I don't want to tell you the rest. Sweden went too far, and so have I. But the Swedes un-derstood what I would like to express, what I try to express. Their welcome was one of the most touching I have had. The entire Swedish Academy was invited to my performances, and the en-tire Swedish Academy came. Over there, they nicknamed me the "angel of the Negro race." It's a little too much; I'm not at all an angel, and it makes me feel embarrassed, even more so to repeat it to you, but wasn't it kind of them?

Sweden and Norway, two beautiful, white countries with lakes scattered everywhere and decorated with blue mountains that sometimes look like glass. As for Denmark, it's completely flat, but like everywhere in Scandinavia, they love Paris and France so much.

Oh, I almost forgot! In these countries, they eat well, lots of cream, and everyone is very, very educated.

Like it or not, every new country enlightens and changes the trav-eler a little; they're open to unexpected sights, they appreciate the hidden song of a new language and a landscape of souls they haven't met before—at least, only indirectly, only in a way that always distorts the truth, the most subtle parts of the truth, the most fragile parts, the parts that make it what it is, the parts that are hardest to translate and explain . . .

That is what I'm trying to explain, Monsieur Sauvage. I can feel it very strongly, yes, but I can't explain it to you. I would need to sing about it or dance. In the beginning, a new country is a new type of music for me, and by the time I leave, it's a dance I would like to try . . . So many dances of my travels with this belt, or rather, necklace of names that I find so funny: Joséphina, Giuseppina, La Bakerova, Koséfina, Phifine . . . and even Pepel, like they said in Vienna. Why Pepel? But the fact they're kind is enough, wouldn't you say? From one European country to the next, I learned to know and understand France better by comparison and the mysterious and very beautiful role that Paris played . . .

Paris is the star of the West, a star, don't you think? A polestar . . .

That reminds me: I forgot to tell you two stories about the North. The first is that one afternoon in Copenhagen, the king asked me to dance just for the little princesses, in a drawing room in the palace. They were so happy, the little princesses, pretty, blonde, rosy girls who were laughing and clapping their hands. They sat in a circle around me, on cushions, on a very old thick rug. But I was even happier than those little girls because to me, you know, all little boys are kings and all little girls are princesses. There is nothing more beautiful or more regal in this world than a child, wouldn't you say? A tantrum makes a prince of any child. And out of all men, my favorites are kings. I would love to read a history of kings everywhere written for children everywhere . . . I am just a working artist, nothing more, who has a duty to dancing and the stage. I couldn't allow myself to have a child or children. Not yet . . . That's what makes me sad. That's also why I love baby animals so much. If you want, I'll tell you the story of all my animals one day.

My other story of the North is a story about a dog, actually. We were in a boat with Pepito, my manager—one day I'll tell you about how much I owe to Pepito—from Denmark to Scandinavia. Now, it's important to realize you can't bring dogs into Sweden. Absolutely forbidden. But I had my dog Phyllis with me, and her husband, who was as fat as a coconut.

The ship's captain told me, "Madame, you'll have to leave your dogs behind if you want to enter Sweden."

I replied, "Captain, I have never left anyone behind and certainly not a dog. Either my dogs come with me or I won't enter at all."

Imagine the situation that put the captain in and how panicked the impresario was. They had to telegram the ministers— imagine this!—the ministers of agriculture and hygiene, again and again, the only ones allowed to decide on such things. Finally, after a good number of strategic telegrams, I was granted permission—a passport—for my dogs, as long as I promised never to let them out of my hotel room. Isn't that cruel? But as you can very well imagine, I did take my dogs out. Phyllis was pregnant at the time. She needed fresh air. And so every day I would wake up at five in the morning to take the dogs for a nice walk. Then Phyllis had her little ones. That morning, while I was walking the other dog, I was caught by a policeman—actually, I ran off when he saw me. I quickly went back to my room, but naturally, the dogs started barking as loudly as they could . . . The policeman knocked on the door and charged in.

"Are your dogs declared?"

"Yes, sir."

"Admitted?"

"Yes, sir."

"How many?"

"Two, sir."

"And those?" the policeman asked, gesturing toward Phyllis's newborns. They were only as big as plums. "Are they not dogs?"

"No," I replied. "Well, barely. As you can see, they're still learning the ropes. You wouldn't want me to put them back in the place they just came out of, I hope, Mr. Policeman sir?"

What a business! The policeman didn't take it well. He woke up all the hotel staff to question them: the managers, the director, the owner. They were this close, Monsieur Sauvage, to waking the minister of agriculture . . . Poor Phyllis . . . I laughed so much afterward!

Romania

From Budapest to Bucharest.

This is where it started to heat up.

In central Europe and Germany, and it would happen in South America, too, I was—without my say, as you can imagine—used either as a warning sign or a "flag" by different political factions. Everything is fair game for politics and politicians, I suppose, I didn't know at the time. But now I have my own two cents on the subject. It's funny and sad at the same time. The old Catholic groups hounded me with their Christian hate, from station to station, from town to town, from one stage to the next. People fought and clashed and got injured. Hundreds, no, thousands of policemen and soldiers had to be called in. In Vienna—even in Vienna, you understand, which is a sister to Paris in many ways—in Vienna they rang all the city's bells at full peal to warn the churchgoers that Josephine Baker, the demon of immorality, the devil herself, had arrived. In central Europe, I saw policemen charging with their swords drawn, and men running past me holding guns . . . I will never forget it. Neither will I forget that there were leaders stupid enough to get worked up over *me*, and my dancing and my freedom, for reasons I didn't and will never understand at all.

None of this, you see, stops me from saying my prayers every evening from the bottom of my heart, or from praying earnestly for all the people who think I'll never be anything more than a poor little black girl who dances like the devil.

Plus, all of this turned my love for France into a wiser love. There you have it.

But let's talk about beautiful, welcoming Romania. Romanians adore France. So I had a weakness for Romanians.

The Eforia Theater, June 1928.

In Bucharest, only very rich people own cars.

I immediately noticed that all the coachmen had lovely feminine faces and quiet voices, very quiet and soft voices . . . It was something! Yes, Monsieur, all these coachmen were eunuchs.

They were dressed like Russians, with enormous sleeves and panels of embroidery everywhere, and small collars and tall hats.

In Bucharest they thought I was a Gypsy. Because there are Gypsies everywhere in that country. They walk around barefoot and make all their anklets jingle, but Gypsies are much darker than me.

On some streets, you'd walk past cows, pigs, goats, rabbits, chickens. And what a smell! In the hotels, you'd also find lots of fleas and other insects that are a little fatter, with more or less of a belly and any number of legs.

But you should really see the Romanian officers. They are wonders . . . Chic, chic, and so well made up. They could give makeup lessons to any European or American actor.

Also in Romania were the most beautiful strawberries, the biggest and sweetest I had ever seen.

And the impresario with the cracking nose, he was also in Romania. Let me tell you how he made me perform in the rain, that kind man, in the torrential rain.

His name was Tănase, Monsieur Tănase, the most famous man in Romania because of his nose. Yes, the ridge of his nose was so big and funny, and such a chameleon feature, that it was almost sad. But what luck, for the father of a family . . . He'd recognize his children right away, wouldn't he? Oh, I swear to you, we recognized the little Tănases right away, because this good impresario had two little Tănases who were blessed in the same way, each one with a nose worth three noses. But that didn't stop them from behaving well, those children. They always followed their father like little dogs. Although there was no danger of losing sight of him . . . Can you imagine those three big noses standing next to each other? Forgive me, I'm being silly, but it was so funny, really so funny . . .

And it was blazing hot!

I performed in Ploieşti, an adorable little town. I saw little girls and little boys walking along, and women carrying baskets of rose petals in each hand. It smelled good, it was cheerful. I thought there must be some sort of flower battle happening there every day. I asked somebody and they said, "Oh no, ma'am, it's to make jam."

In Romania they also use rose petals to make compote. It's excellent, extremely excellent, actually.

Everyone was dripping with sweat, and everyone was applauding. I had to extend my run: they really looked so happy to see me dancing, the Romanians in Ploieşti. Like children who couldn't stop laughing.

The stage was lit with oil lamps that were lifted and lowered and lifted again. And it smelled like kerosene! And it was hot! A very small stage: I could hear the two men, standing on each side, huffing and puffing as they pulled the curtain.

But the musicians are extraordinary in Romania; they're jugglers, they're acrobats. They hit impossible notes with their bows and slide trombones.

And they are affectionate, and they are sweet.

They envelop you, tie you in with threads of music that they know how to spin so well, lulling themselves, lulling their instruments, eyes closed, eyebrows arched high, until it becomes the most delicate, the sweetest sound . . .

Now let me take you back to the Cărăbuş Theater in Bucharest. It was my farewell evening. And it was still blazing hot!

It was an open-air theater.

The stars were hidden behind heavy, black clouds.

Lightning started winking in the distance.

The heat was unbearable.

Cărăbuş Theater has seventeen hundred seats. That evening, it held three thousand spectators.

Monsieur Tănase was on edge. He wouldn't stop looking at the sky. The little Tănases were watching their father anxiously. A storm was coming; disaster, too. Because, remember, the audience would have to be reimbursed if it rained before the halfway point of the show. And Monsieur Tănase, who took pride in doing things well, had invested an enormous amount of money. He was also scared that the storm might panic the three thousand spectators; that they might break everything, before crushing each other.

It was a rushed show. The orchestra skipped over half the notes. The tenor shoved aside the magician, who swallowed the tightrope walker, who fell right into the comedy routine.

The first drop of rain, an enormous, tragic drop, fell onto the conductor's head. He leaped five feet into the air and set the orchestra off, who started playing at full tilt. The race was on: we had to make it halfway through the show.

Then before you knew it, splat, splat, splat. Huge drops started hammering down left and right. Monsieur Tănase went pale; his children were going crazy. They were running through the auditorium, through the wings. Mr. Tănase was moaning, "I'm ruined, children, ruined!"

All the while, splat, splat, the prelude to the downpour.

They killed the running order, and I went onstage. But the candy jar I was meant to climb into was deeper than I thought and . . . Crash! I tumbled inside it as if down a well. We had to close the curtain. I reappeared in front of it. The raindrops redoubled. Hundreds of umbrellas were opening in front of me, and I saw hundreds of women lifting their skirts over their heads.

With the first step of my dance, the storm suddenly let loose. Poor Monsieur Tănase! Never mind the rain! I decided to keep dancing.

I danced with an umbrella.

The musicians were all playing while holding umbrellas.

It was out of tune! It was crazy! And the thunderclaps, oh, là là . . .

Half the audience ran away during the shower. People were getting their money back at the exit. But luckily, other people who'd been waiting outside for who knows what, because there'd been no space left, were rushing in, rushing in anyway, to see Josephine.

By that point I had closed my umbrella and was dancing like I was in an aquarium. My banana belt was soaked with water. The soggy bananas started falling off, plop, plop, onto the ground.

The new audience went wild with joy.

My hair pomade and makeup were running into my eyes.

I was wearing feathers, too: I looked pitiful, like a poor wet little chicken, soaked through and flailing.

But the orchestra kept going and got more and more out of tune. What do you expect? They were drowning, too, down in their pit. Water was gurgling in the horns, sloshing inside the cellos. The bass drum was getting droopier by the second.

"Stop! Stop! No more refunds!" shouted Monsieur Tănase, with the two little Tănases following behind, dripping as they scurried along.

And it rained and rained!

And Josephine kept dancing, Monsieur Sauvage. It was her farewell night.

Despite the rain, all the opera glasses were fixed on me. We forgot about the rain, we carried on, I carried on, we all carried on against the storm. What an audience, my friend! What enthusiasm. And what a storm . . . What a bath!

That's all for Romania!

Czechoslovakia

Really? I haven't told you about my airplane journeys yet? An airplane is like a cradle with wings, or a swing, don't you think? The engine rumbles, it's warm, so I fall asleep. I sleep . . . My memories of airplanes are memories of dreams. I never saw anything, I just slept. Paris to the Netherlands, Rotterdam to Amsterdam, Paris to London . . . Actually, I remember Paris to London very well, in the fog. The whitish fog, the big patches that would clear from time to time, drifting, fading away, uncovering a field or village below. And then the sea, a cloudy, wrinkled mirror, and then the yellow and black fog, too, and sleeping behind the engine that would rumble quietly, keep on rumbling . . . When one is asleep, one doesn't see the people vomiting, which is a plus. I also like boats a lot because of that same rocking feeling that—I can't help myself—makes me start singing one of those old spirituals from South Carolina, an old spiritual that puts me to sleep . . . So I become both my own nanny and my own child. I love all hours of sleep. Do you know anything sweeter than sleep, any images more extraordinary, more frightening, or more soothing than the ones we find in sleep? I feel that we always sing, we artists, to calm something inside the audience that needs soothing, something that needs to be released into dreams . . .

I'll talk to you later about boats and the time I crossed the line with Monsieur Le Corbusier, the architect. I know every train car in Europe and both Americas, too. The ones in North America, I got to know them when I was just a little showgirl . . . I can picture myself in a corner of one of those big cars with my little bundle and teensy hat. And the ones in South America . . . Ah! Wait, here's a story they used to tell in Argentina. The scene takes place on a station platform, of course.

EMPLOYEE (*taking off his cap and scratching his ear*): Will you
    be crossing the Andes, miss?
JOSEPHINE BAKER: Yes, sir.
EMPLOYEE (*serious but with some hesitation*): Ah! Ah . . .
    And . . . did they tell you?

JOSEPHINE: Tell me what?

EMPLOYEE (*increasingly serious, polite, and cold*): Not to travel in the last car?

JOSEPHINE: No . . . Why?

EMPLOYEE: Because, miss, the trains that cross the Andes are very long and very fast, and the last car shakes terribly. It's not pleasant.

JOSEPHINE (*widening her big, bright eyes*): But, sir, in that case, why not remove the last car?

It's nicely done, isn't it! The Argentinians had a lot of fun with this little story. It made its way around all the streets and pampas . . . But please, remind me, we weren't in the pampas but still in Central Europe. I was arriving in Prague, I think. Yes . . . Prague.

Did you know the Eiffel Tower had a child? That it can have babies, tower babies? It has a child in Prague, opposite the Royal Palace, a little thing sixty meters tall. They call it Petřín . . . But let's slow down; I've only just arrived.

In Prague, the city of a hundred towers and four hundred domes, they know how to host. It's fantastic, wonderful, amazing. The station was thronging, the platforms were swarming with people; all around the station it was swarming with people . . . I'm not scared of theater crowds: that is simply a duel one has to win. I square my shoulders and my heart becomes hard as a fist . . . But here, for the first time, I was scared of the crowd, of its curiosity, its affection, its enthusiasm. I was drowning in warmth and friendship . . . How would I leave the train? How would I find my way? I held on to Pepito and Pepito held on to me, so he wouldn't lose me. The stationmaster came toward us in his full uniform as grand marshal of the trains and started singing my praises. My foot had barely touched the platform when—my, oh my—there was a tremendous surge in the crowd. I was holding a bouquet of flowers in the national colors in my left hand. This bouquet was snatched away, torn to pieces, annihilated in less than a minute. I turned around right away; Pepito had disappeared, swept away by the crowd.

I was alone in a sea of raised hands holding on to hats. It was utterly crazy. I wanted to laugh and cry. I was like a cork stopper out on the water. I didn't know what to hold on to or what to say. Suddenly, I found myself in an old hackney coach, so old, so old and so pitiful. The horse and the coachman must have lived three hundred years between them. Meanwhile, the crowd had surrounded the carriage that was officially waiting for me. Even so, I thought they were going to crush me in this old hackney coach with the old coachman who didn't understand a word, but then the old horse started to move, one step at a time. I was in little pieces in that old coach.

Happy and awestruck.

Prague is clean, majestic, and austere.

There is an old bridge that you are not meant to laugh at. It is beautiful, ancient, and there are dozens of legends about it, each one more surprising than the last. It's called Charles Bridge. Monsieur Poodle-Head, our manager, told us about it:

"The Charles Bridge was built by Emperor Charles the Fourth, who was raised in the French court. He changed his name from

Wenceslas to that of Charles. The Charles Bridge connects the Old Town, with its university and marketplace, to the area of Malá Strana, home to the old Czech aristocracy, artists, and—forgive me, miss—and to those delightful sinning women."

Wow!

That Monsieur Poodle-Head really meant business as our guide. That's why I remember his patter. But the story of how the bridge was built is even funnier.

To make the Charles Bridge stronger, the contractor decided to mix the lime and mortar with eggs. So it was decided, in agreement with the government, that every town in the country would send cartfuls of fresh eggs to Prague, to build the bridge. Can you imagine the size of the omelet? Now, one small town wanted to set itself apart from the others even though it wasn't very rich. The townsfolk thought about it and guess what . . . They sent a cartful of hard-boiled eggs! Now, what was that little town called? I can't remember the name, how silly. A crazy name, as crazy as the contractor himself.

Have you ever seen it rain rabbit's feet, Monsieur Sauvage?

I have, personally, onstage in Prague. But it's goose that's the national dish of Czechoslovakia. The countryside is white with them, white with geese, like snow or giant cauliflowers with feet. They eat them with little dumplings instead of vegetables. They have goose on every menu, goose with every meal. There are geese in every house. On Sundays, the country folk eat a goose.

Anyway, back to the rain of rabbit's feet. It happened in Prague, on the enormous stage at the enormous Lucerna, and it's all your fault, Monsieur Sauvage. You wrote about it, didn't you? That I had a lucky rabbit's foot that I adored and never let out of my sight. And so, to make me happy and to make sure I would always be lucky, the audience in Prague—who can read French very well, by the way—one evening they threw hundreds and hundreds of rabbit's feet at me, of all colors and sizes. A wagonload of rabbit's feet.

If I had known, I would have brought back a few for you, the freshest ones, as a thank-you and as payback. I know you probably don't need such things, since all those fantasies in your head come true anyway. But you know, my dear, I really do have a lucky rabbit's foot—I even have one or two spares.

✦ ✦ ✦

And then disaster struck. Orchestras, Monsieur Sauvage, can be deadly.

There I was, onstage at Lucerna—which means "lantern." It's one of the biggest theaters in Europe, definitely the biggest one underground. The Lucerna theater can hold up to eight thousand people.

It was full that night.

While I looked at the vast expanse of the stalls, feeling a little afraid, I thought about what someone had told me: that those eight thousand people could be drowned in a matter of minutes. Because the enormous pipe that provided water for the whole city of Prague happened to pass just above the theater! All it would take was one leak, one crack, and the panic and the drowning wouldn't be far behind. I couldn't help looking up at the ceiling, but there was no water dripping and no damp spot growing above my head.

A gigantic, rectangular, cold theater. I couldn't see the back of it. Two long rows of grand boxes on either side.

A theater that made its actors curiously small; that soaked up their voices; that wore them out, made them fade, lost them . . .

I felt lost.

The manager—whom I call Monsieur Poodle-Head because of his thick, curly hair—wore a small diamond badge of a lantern in his buttonhole, and the other staff wore a small metal one in theirs: it was the theater's symbol.

Lucerna, what a long, deep, and cold theater! I really did not feel comfortable. I instinctively looked around for someone to reassure me. Nobody. But then I imagined I was standing on the mysterious Alchemists' Lane and in front of the Stations of the Cross in the park and in the Old Jewish Cemetery. Suddenly, the legend of the Golem, a zombie created by a chief rabbi, a great wizard, came to mind. Not what you'd usually think of when you're trying to pluck up some courage.

I shook all that off and thought to myself, "Come on, you've got to succeed."

I know how to toughen up when I need to succeed.

It wasn't very long ago that I'd been singing on a stage and my voice wasn't very strong. I heard it get lost in the distance, dissipate through the heavy silence hanging over that gigantic, underground theater. The first patches of applause did me good, but that was loose cannon fire: it didn't get far; it hardly spread through the thousands of spectators in the audience.

And then the orchestra launched into the music for my dance.

"Now," I thought, "the worst has passed. I'm saved."

At first everything went swimmingly. I did my best to cover

the entire stage with my steps, dancing all the way to the right and all the way to the left. Then I noticed that the orchestra was gradually getting faster. I looked at the conductor. He didn't seem concerned down there in the pit. His nose was lit up from underneath, and his white hands, his ghostly hands, were moving this way and that like he was trying to swat notes like invisible flies around the musicians' heads . . . And the music was speeding up, and speeding up a bit more . . . I danced faster to stay in time and tried to catch the conductor's attention. When I passed in front of him, I stamped my foot. He just looked at me with wide eyes. He hadn't understood, this man; he didn't understand. And now his arms were moving at a terrifying pace. But I kept dancing to the rhythm he was forcing on me. Sweat ran down my body, drops fell from the end of my nose, my hands lost track.

I went even closer to the conductor and shouted, "Too quickly, too quickly!"

Either my words disappeared into the music or the conductor didn't understand me. So I shouted again: "Too quickly, too quickly, *trop vite, trop vite!*"

It was crazy, but I rose to the challenge and danced like I *was* crazy. Suddenly I slipped, fell on my side, but I leaped to my feet again. I had grazed the entire side of my arm and my elbow. I felt my blood mixing in with my sweat, running down to my fingertips. At the same time, I heard a thunder of applause: the audience thought my fall was part of the act . . .

I yelled one last time: "Trop vite! Trop vite!"

But the conductor simply looked at me like a lunatic and set the frantic musicians off at full speed. I felt dizzy; I dropped to my knees, but only for a second. Then I gritted my teeth and said to myself, "If you stop, it's all over. You have to dance. You have to wear out the orchestra and that monster of a conductor!"

My knees were bleeding. Blood was running all the way down my legs. I was like a dancer who'd been skinned alive, blood all over me. I danced like a demon, I danced and danced and danced; I spun and leaped and ran. The whirlwind of music tried to sweep me away—I was stronger.

"If you give up, it'll be on your head," I thought.

I didn't give up. Finally, the conductor dropped his arm and the orchestra seemed to deflate, to suddenly fall flat. The thousands of faces in that gigantic Lucerna spun around me. Everything went red, as if it were on fire. I heard a deep rumble, like a storm breaking, and I collapsed, sunk right to the bottom of my tiredness, my exhaustion, my pain.

I was burning like a flame.

The audience cheered and clamored but it was no use. The curtain wasn't raised again. I was unconscious. They took me to my dressing room. I was out cold. I bled quietly on the ground, into a rug, my arms wrapped around me.

Austria

Vienna is in the middle of Austria, a country that doesn't seem big enough to keep its capital flourishing.

It is a very big city, beautiful and vibrant: Paris's sister.

If Prague has a small Eiffel Tower, then Vienna has a big wheel that looks just like the one we used to have here in Paris in the past. But the first thing you notice when you arrive in Vienna is, once again, the coachmen: enormous, jolly coachmen on little carriages. Coachmen bigger than their carriages, unbelievably wide coachmen—and their manners!

To them, it's very simple: all their clients must be archdukes and emperors, so they bow and salute to the left, right, in front, and behind with the full breadth of their shoulders and their bellies.

Vienna is the city of romance and *lieder.*

But consider the Danube, the beautiful blue Danube. It's much less blue than the Seine.

I got remarkable press before I arrived in Vienna. Firstly, thanks to a politician, a Czech politician—there are half a million Czechs in Vienna—called Monsieur Jerzabek. Pardon me, but they told me that in French, Jerzabek means "little crane"—the bird with long legs or the steam engine with the very long neck.

Monsieur Jerzabek led a magnificent campaign against me. He even took it to Parliament—I'd never have expected it, Monsieur Sauvage, absolutely unexpected.

And so, thanks to Monsieur Jerzabek and without my say, I came to represent the "moral decadence threatening the great country of Austria."

Secondly, thanks to Jesuit Reverend Father Frey, who only knew me through the stupidest and most unsavory tales, I also represented Lust itself.

This happened, as I said, before I arrived in Austria. Despite everything, they couldn't ban me from entering Vienna. But thanks to that publicity, it wasn't a dancer the city was expecting but a demon—the Black Demon, the heretic incarnate.

When I arrived in Vienna, all the city's bells were ringing, to warn the churchgoers that if I walked by, they should run the other way and hide in their most secret retreats until I left the city. On every street corner they handed out the most hateful leaflets against me: "May this woman, Immorality herself, be punished as she deserves." Well, I can't deny there were lots of people and plenty of the best kind, too, I believe, to welcome Immorality herself, despite the warning bells and the little pieces of paper. That's because Viennese men are charming and the women are sweet. I got to know Viennese women a little later on: they are exceptionally elegant, delicate, loving, not to mention very romantic and—the best thing, as far as the men are concerned—not the least bit jealous.

Parisian women and Viennese women, the two wonders of Europe, Monsieur Sauvage.

Even so, my police guard in Vienna was like none I've seen since: an army of policemen, serious, straight-faced, and attentive, like butlers.

But I should make a few things clear. First, our visit with *La Revue Blanc et Noir* came at a bad time: a time of crisis and unemployment. The ticket prices were very high, too high. Maybe the angry crowd waiting outside the theater doors every night to protest were mostly protesting because they couldn't afford to come inside. Plus, during the show, we were wrong to have included a parade of models—"queens of America and the Queen of Paradise," according to the program—wearing luxury dresses that cost twenty-five thousand francs each. Hungry people hate waste, hate being made fun of, and hate any implication that we might be mocking them, don't they? And they're absolutely right . . . But none of it was my fault and there was nothing I could do. The dollar is no god of mine.

The last time Reverend Father Frey went up to the pulpit at St. Paul's—just next door to the Johann Strauss Theater, where I was performing—the church was full. It was the day before I arrived. Everyone was waiting for him to start ranting. But he didn't. Sorrowfully, he described me as simply the icon of our sinful times. In fact, in his sweet voice, the good father pinned all the sins of old Europe on me. Why thank you, Father. Everyone is allowed to make mistakes.

In fact, repentance—this at least I was taught, even if nothing else, in a little school in a little American chapel in St. Louis, with a few other children all different shades of black, but very pious—repentance has opened many doors for the most desperate sinners.

The evening of that very day, however, when Father Frey was mainly preaching against "white Negroes"—Europeans and those Viennese who dared to dance the Charleston—that evening the Johann Strauss Theater, which is opposite St. Paul's, was also full, full to the brim, with the exact same people, of course, men and women.

They were waiting for the devil to speak . . .

I made a very simple entrance onto the stage. There was a second of complete silence and surprise. Then I sang with all my heart, with my whole, trembling, beating heart. I sang "Sleep, My Poor Baby," an old Negro spiritual from back in the slave times, when Negroes were good for nothing but dying from exhaustion and despair after being beaten by their very Christian owners.

Forgive me, but it really felt like the entire theater was collapsing . . .

When the cheering and applause died down, I danced like I always have and always will, not thinking about good or evil but only about my dance, my honest and ever so pure dance, to show humankind and God—who I've been assured is the God of all people whether they're white, black, yellow, or red—that there is a youthfulness that is free, eternal and forever, in spite of everything, a great and simple joie de vivre that's enough in itself.

Write that down, Monsieur Sauvage, and make sure you emphasize that the Black Demon, the little black girl, the pickaninny, says her prayers every night when she gets home after dancing, no matter how tired she is.

By now the Austrians had accepted me, adopted me. I think they liked me a lot. I also found a man in Vienna, a good and generous practicing Catholic who bravely and passionately defended me, the most eccentric man in Central Europe: Count Sternberg. After the revolution and the nobility reforms, this is what he had engraved on his business card:

CHARLEMAGNE GAVE ME A TITLE.
A BLACKSMITH'S SON TOOK IT FROM ME.

Count Sternberg was coming from Geneva as I arrived in Vienna.

He wanted to give a lecture about the League of Nations and a speech about me, both in the same evening. I told you he was eccentric. I'll never forget it . . .

The whole of Vienna was there, all low necklines and dark suits, the nobility and the bourgeoisie. The world has always considered it scandalous to be eccentric and outspoken. Before, people couldn't stand it; now it's fashionable.

The first part of the evening was about Geneva and the second part about me. Count Sternberg—a man full of memories and anecdotes, a man who was never at a loss for words—gave the hypocrites a good talking-to. Here are some of the things he said that I happen to remember. They made the audience gasp a little:

Ladies and gentlemen, the League of Nations is a club for giant stomachs and minuscule brains.

If Christ returned, the Europeans would unite with the Americans to nail him to a cross of pure gold.

He also said this:

On the night of a great speech against alcohol, a lavish banquet was held in Geneva. In front of each guest were a dozen glasses for the wines. When it was time for dessert, yet more small glasses were brought out, this time for the liqueurs. There were nine types of liqueurs. The abstainers did not refuse any of it. Here you see the limited reach of politicians' moralizing behavior.

Besides, what is the use of banning wine on one hand and praising Christ on another? Did he not turn water into wine at Cana? Is that not sufficient guidance? If only he had done the opposite! As you can see, we interpret the Gospels as we like, and that is a tragedy. Nevertheless, it is written in the Gospels, in the simplest language in the world, that Jesus turned water into wine.

"Josephine Baker is an example of our times, one of the most outstanding examples." That is what the Count said next.

After which he gave me several compliments, but I don't need to repeat them. Among them, the following struck me the most—not that I'm trying to use any of this to my advantage. Let everyone judge for themselves:

Whites don't know how to dance. Whoever wants to know and admire the profound and enchanting art of dance should make their way to Asia or Africa, among colored people. Only they—colored people—have been able to preserve the human quality and sacred nature of dance: from the facial expression of comedy or tragedy to ritual movements that draw and hold the attention of gods and demons.

The highest ideal of human art is, and has always been, the nude woman. And that part of the nude woman that scares Monsieur Jerzabek has always been depicted fearlessly in true art. Besides, the one who fights against nudity blasphemes against God—who created man naked.

Can you believe the Holy Church is afraid of something so

small? I suggest you go to St. Peter's in Rome and lift your eyes to the sky of nude figures painted on the vault. It is a heavenly ideal of nude figures.

The most daring nude figures that one can set eyes on in this world are in the Pope's house . . . So why are these priests campaigning against Josephine Baker? Clearly, they were not taught correctly about good and evil. The Vatican is silently condemning poor, tormented Negro priests, and to what purpose?

Female beauty reaches its peak through dance.

Belly dancing was performed by the first Christians in Arabia, in Palestine. Did this "damned" dance stop the Copts from being the most devout followers of the Catholic Church?

I do not see how natural nudity could compromise morality. But history has some suggestions: Queen Margot used to dress with her breasts uncovered because she had beautiful breasts. However, Henry IV's second wife, Marie de Medici, who had drooping breasts, had women's necklines raised up to their noses . . .

Count Sternberg was very successful; he was the best kind; and thanks to him my victory in Vienna was complete. I could walk around the city without the bells ringing, and I made the most of it. I strolled at my leisure around the beautiful avenues where the emperor and his entourage of highly decorated officers seemed to have left a big void.

Every evening I danced at the Wolf's Pavilion, the chicest cabaret in Vienna, with my Paris jazz band.

During the day, I was a tourist.

I saw Schönbrunn and its gardens. And the story of the eagle, what a wonderful story! And the St. Stephen church, a perfect example of the oldest Austrian tradition. What a picturesque church.

The cafés there don't have terraces but they are very lively.

Wiener schnitzel . . .

Viennese coffee . . .

Schlagsahne, that's good, strong coffee with whipped cream, very sweet and light . . . Oh, là là, a dream for the tongue! The Viennese love it so much, they made an opera about it.

That's all for Austria.

Hungary

At the station in Budapest, I was met by a row of film cameras; a row of soldiers with their swords drawn; a row of policemen holding guns . . .

I went to Budapest twice, in 1928 and 1929. I went incognito the second time so I wouldn't upset everyone and so I wouldn't have to be followed by swords and guns, which I've never had any affection for. But I do have strange memories of Budapest.

It was in Budapest that I believed the Danube could be blue.

In any case, that's where it's the biggest and most majestic and most beautiful. When you arrive, you see a gigantic bronze eagle appearing over the top of a steep cliff. In the shadow of its wings lies the city, the Queen of the Danube, each of her two halves as enchanting as the other: Buda and Pest, with all the harsh memories of their history—oh, I love stories from history!

But first, I want to talk to you about Hungarian violins. Pages and pages should be written about the violins of Hungary and the songs of Hungary. Budapest may well be the romantic capital of Europe. You really must listen to those Hungarian violins quivering, so soft and lively, at sunset, a royal sunset when the golden Danube with its wonderful bridges is like a sparkling train behind the sun.

Budapest is the city that gave me my best and worst welcomes, you know, the city that touched me most deeply. That's why I wanted to speak in Hungarian and sing and perform in it. I probably didn't have a perfect accent or follow the rules, but it was my little tribute.

And so, in the Royal Orpheum, I performed a sketch, a real play, *Le Masque Bleu,* by Árpád Pásztor.

But wait, that was my second visit.

The first visit—I've already told you about the security convoy I had—I owed my life to a big oxcart that I hid in, right in the middle of the crowd, like a fort. The Hungarians didn't dare climb it. But they did tear my dress to pieces to try and get a souvenir. They wanted to see me naked. They went a bit far, those Hungarians . . . And you'll soon see they even went a little further. First, my visit was debated in Parliament three times. They didn't want me, the "Black Demon," as they had just been calling me in Vienna.

Before anything else, I had to put on a private performance for a censorship board chaired by a government minister. What do you think happened? Well! It went splendidly. I had to do an encore for the censorship board. And the minister even thought I was wearing a little too much!

"I'll be fine here," I thought.

And I explored Budapest as I pleased.

In the middle of the city, two hundred and thirty-five meters high, is a rock: Gellért Hill. It's absolutely full of fantastic caves. And there is a belt of hot springs running all the way around it. Budapest is a city of baths. Whichever side you are on, you'll come across bathhouses with bubbling water and marble columns, and marble statues, and flowers growing on Roman terraces.

Their Champs-Élysées is called Andrássy út.

The Royal Orpheum, where I was performing, is on the corner of Elizabeth Boulevard. On the steps of all the theaters, at both the entrance and the exit, you will find peasant women in the national dress, very colorful. They sell handmade embroidery; it really is astonishing. Why don't we all wear Hungarian embroidery all the time? Leaves, vines, arabesques, ornate frogging . . .

The Orpheum's auditorium was full.

As I started dancing, there was a strange hubbub.

I looked up and suddenly saw a man leaning over the side of the gallery. He was holding something. He threw it into the middle of the auditorium . . . A bomb! For one endless second I had goosebumps under my ostrich feathers.

I closed my eyes . . .

It was just an ammonia bomb. Even so, you can imagine the situation, the fear. By some miracle, nobody panicked. But the bomb did fall onto a woman's leg, and she was injured and quite badly burned.

"Hungarians really go all out," I thought to myself. "They're so sweet . . ."

And I carried on dancing.

Oh yes! The sweet violins playing on terraces with that strange view, that grand view, of the bridges in the distance. By the way, the oldest bridge is the suspended bridge. It's supported on each side by big stone lions. Apparently, once the sculptor had finished his tremendous job, he realized that his lions, his big stone lions that had given him so much trouble and should have been his life's masterpiece, had no tongues. The sculptor had forgotten to give his lions tongues. He was in so much despair, he stood on top of the bridge and shot himself in the head. They found his body on the shores of Margaret Island, which is one big rose garden.

The Hungarian Parliament Building is the biggest one in Europe, with pointed steeples everywhere and a huge dome on top that has a pointed steeple, too.

To the right of the Danube, following its lazy current, is Buda, with the Old Town and the mountain. To the left is Pest, the plain and the shops. On one side, an enormous castle and the white towers of another monument; on the other, its counterpart, the Parliament. Opposite the royal castle is the Corso, Gypsies, and elegant, lively, multicolored lives. Bathhouses and violins everywhere.

I don't know why, but Hungarians remind me of Spaniards.

They eat lunch very late, and everything is made with lard and paprika. The chicken with bright red paprika: excellent. The crepes with walnuts or jam: excellent, too. Even better with a violin playing in the background.

Unfortunately for me, the first time I arrived in Budapest was at the height of a wave of prudishness, after the revolutionary wave. That explained the ammonia bomb incident and the tears, the tears, a flood of them in that theater . . . a whole theater watching me through their tears.

The second time, I took to the stage with a bouquet made of the national colors of Hungary. There was a Frenchwoman in the theater: Mistinguett. I wanted us all to applaud France by applauding Mistinguett, and we gave away all the flowers in my bouquet.

In *Le Masque Bleu* I played the comedy role of a maid. Under my tiny petticoat, I was wearing trousers with lace so big it looked like the teeth of a saw or stalactites. Every time I bent over you saw my lovely lace, and every time the audience would burst out laughing. In the play, I was looking after a sick child while dreaming of going to a society party. As soon as the child fell asleep, I put on my mistress's shoes, dress, coat, and hat. I was ready, I was hobbling, I was ridiculous and magnificent. The child woke up, of course. He had a fever, he was delirious. So we just pretended we were there, both of us, at this party. He clutched the useless invitation in his little hand. I felt guilty, and I held him and told him about it . . . That was all, but it was so much fun! I performed in Hungarian and with all my heart. The applause was deafening . . .

Oh, Hungary! It was the first time in my life I acted in a play and the first time I acted in a foreign language, you know.

Spain

Combs as tall as skyscrapers, castanets, orange trees, spiders, penitents wearing pointed hoods of all colors, bulls, big hats, wrought-iron bars on all the windows, courtyards with fountains, other things, very nice journalists—really very nice—and blue, white, very deep snow. That's Spain.

What can I say . . . When I arrived in Madrid it was covered in snow. It wasn't really the Spaniards' fault, but I was disappointed. I had expected to find flowers on every balcony and the sun shining on every flower. Luckily, it didn't last long: the snowmen were killed off within twenty-four hours.

Spain is probably the country I know the best in Europe. I stayed there for several months. I performed in every town and city . . . Spain feels like a faraway country, almost a small village, cut off from great, modern machines. But it has such an unbelievable variety, so many original beauties: the men, the women, the dancing, and what splendid rice! Cooked Valencia style, with peppers, shrimp, mussels, and chicken. I ate it till I was sick.

No, three hundred American lobsters still can't beat rice the way they do it in Valencia.

But I don't know how to talk to you about Spain. It's a dream. It has wonderful and unfamiliar music, with cities like private mansions, filigreed archways, shady gardens with scents that make your head spin, and churches even shadier than the gardens, even cooler and more scented, with lots of candles.

Shall we take it one city at a time?

Madrid—I first performed in a theater on the outskirts, then at the Gran Metropolitano, with great success. Naturally, they asked me to watch a bullfight, but I'd prefer to see bulls running around a meadow than an arena—never mind for me, but all the better for them.

Barcelona—A completely unique city, the city of colorful nougat, waterside romances, trade unions, workers, the liveliest in all of Spain.

But they told me: "You're not in Spain here."

Then I sang in Catalan, and so much the better. It was carnival time. I watched the parade. Las Ramblas was glittering with confetti. They threw little colorful balls at me as they went past, and lots of streamers, like lassos . . . I was completely tangled up, blinded, happy, because that's what true happiness is.

I visited all the dance houses in Barcelona and learned just how exceptional dancing could be. That's how I met La Macarrona, who taught Pastora Imperio and La Argentina, a little woman who weighed one hundred and ten kilos, no less! She is the most beautiful, most intelligent, most expressive dancer I have ever had the pleasure of admiring and applauding. Dancing Gypsies aren't women; they are pure rhythm, they are the dances of love, passion, and melancholy themselves, that wild melancholy that is everything in Spain's very character. The Gypsies dance all day and all night long; they don't seem to rest, as if they're fueled by their own dancing, drunk on it.

Before leaving Barcelona I wanted to pay my respects to J. Demon, the composer who wrote the music for my song "Suppose."

Huesca—I finished my performance, I bowed . . . and suddenly, there was a flood, Monsieur Sauvage, a storm of cheers, an avalanche of hats, coats, handkerchiefs, ties, suspenders, flowers, jackets, and even a few pairs of shoes . . . I was heartbroken, overwhelmed, ready to cry. I had done my best. I didn't know this was how they showed enthusiasm in Spain. I was scared. I picked up a shoe and a belt . . . I know you're wondering if I was happy and if I laughed afterward. But in the moment, it wasn't funny to be mistaken for a *toro* . . .

✦　✦　✦

Seville—I stepped off the train and what did I see? Along the streets, everywhere, an enormous Ku Klux Klan gathering: it was Holy Week. High, pointed hoods like sugar loaves. Smoking, crackling, sinister torches. Candles with pale, flickering flames. There was singing to guitars. The penitents had extravagant, luxurious costumes, red aprons, purple masks, yellow sticks, and huge golden crosses on their backs. Many of them were barefoot. Holy statues, with halos like tropical suns, were parading in among the different groups. They made me pay forty pesetas for a seat so I could watch.

Seville is the real Spain, the Spain of legend, where the women wear long, shimmering mantillas.

While I was in Seville, the big Ibero-American Exposition was also taking place. The hotels were full, all the rooms in the city had been rented out, no chance of finding a bed. In the end, I found one with a poor family, but it was at least twenty centimeters too short. It goes without saying that I hardly closed my eyes for the eight nights I spent there. Instead, I listened to the fiery hubbub of Seville on the banks of the Guadalquivir and I watched all the little insects marching in time on the ceiling and walls, racing about, the spiders hunting, the centipedes, the bugs, the ladybirds *and* ladybugs—that room had it all. But that bed, that tiny bed . . . I couldn't take it anymore, so, never mind, I stuck out my feet. Dinnertime, little insects! And a few really did come and tickle me sometimes. Then I would get up and explore Seville, its soft guitars, and the jingling keys of the *serenos*, the night watchmen.

Pamplona—The church was opposite the theater. I'd just paid forty pesetas to watch a religious event in Seville; I thought I had the right to some consideration. Think again! The Catholic Mothers Association launched a long, aggressive petition against me, fittingly antagonistic, signed and sealed . . . But they didn't convince the mayor. I had danced in Madrid without incurring wrath from the heavens or the king . . . So they let me perform, and they enjoyed it. A few heavy hats were thrown my way, and I caught them midair like discuses.

Valladolid—Old capital, old library. They showed me books covered in leather and decorated with ivory and diamonds. There were manuscripts as big as tables, with big, red capital letters, still bleeding.

Málaga, in the middle of a dust bowl; San Sebastián, Oviedo, Santander, Logroño, Gijón . . . I can't list them all, but I do like saying their names, which sound like castanets and jewelry. In Zaragoza, they danced the jota for me. Oh! How enchanting. I would love to dance a jota in a circle of clapping hands. In Valencia, the city of orange trees and flowers, I saw a comedy with singing; it had great rhythm and was as choreographed as a ballet. I ate rice there . . . Let's not talk about it again; I already have . . . But that rice! It's worth the trip for that alone. Big grains of rice with . . . Sorry, let's not talk about it again.

Córdoba, Córdoba, Córdoba . . . It's enough, don't you think, to say its name, to see gardens, palaces, patios with bulging jars and little round trees . . . Córdoba, pretty pictures on smooth, perfumed leather.

That leaves Granada. Orange trees, myrtle and oleander, yews and black cypress, the Arab gardens of the Alhambra and the Generalife palaces, the most beautiful gardens in the world. Roses, carnations, lilac, jasmine, lavender, springs and fountains, fragrances and marble . . . And then, in earthen houses, in holes dug out of the ground, the poor Gypsies, terribly poor, with red, red lips and black-lined eyes, Gypsies who never stop smoking, one cigarette after another, singing love songs in hushed voices to the sound of copper being beaten to a rhythm, from dawn until the evening twilight . . .

Spain is one big ride of unending, maybe endless, fun. I may have danced and sung in all these cities, but for me it was simply a tour of love.

Germany

Germany is the first European country I visited after my early days in France. They welcomed me enthusiastically. If I had accepted the contract that Max Reinhardt offered me at the time—this was in 1926—maybe I could have had an acting career in Germany. But my star was in Paris's sky.

You told me, Monsieur Sauvage, that you liked Germany, the Germany of poets and underground brasseries, the Germany of wonderful machines. But could you understand the German mind? Not me. Germany is a country of order and light—Berlin is one hundred times brighter at night than Paris—but it's in this country of order and comfort that the ghost of suicide is a permanent resident. The first time I was in Germany I met Max Reinhardt, the extraordinary director. The second time, I met the tentative ghost of suicide. I greeted it. And I drank beer.

◆　◆　◆

I couldn't stay in Germany for several months without going back to France two or three times to lift my spirits. This was at the end of 1928. It was at this time—I want you to write this—that I met my best friends.

With them, Pepito and I found a home, a family, and an affection that is still dear to me.

Pure friendship, you see, is a miracle. Right now I have five friends—no, six, maybe seven: an enormous number. You know the seventh: my audience.

Berlin! It was crazy, the first time! A triumph! They made it a triumph for me.

There was a big dance hall. When I went inside, the musicians stopped playing, stood up, and bowed to me.

Berlin is where I received the most love letters, flowers, and gifts.

Max Reinhardt came to see me. He brought a contract with him. "I'll hire you for three years at the Deutsches Theater. You'll become the biggest star in Europe, believe me."

But before I left for Germany, I had already signed a contract with the Folies Bergère.

Neue Kunsthandlung, Tauentzienstrasse, February 6 to 18, 1926: a fancy-dress ball. We were squashed in like sardines: women and men pressed up against each other, Negroes everywhere you looked.

I was on the judging panel. We would give a prize to one lady in costume.

I explored Berlin in the early morning. Berlin looked very French to me, a very beautiful city, clean, light, and well laid out.

In Berlin's magazines and newspapers they wrote that I was the face of contemporary German Expressionism, German Primitivism, things like that.

They are funny.

What does that mean, anyway? I was born in 1906, the twentieth century.

Alles für Josephine.

It got funnier and funnier. And why not?

Now let's talk about the scandal in Berlin. I was performing at the Theater des Westens.

I was to appear in a revue—a bad revue—that had been put together in less than a month. All the publicity revolved around my name, and because of that, I was made responsible for the revue's fate. But a star, whoever she may be, cannot single-handedly save a revue that is ugly, stupid, and pretentious all at once. And so the stupid theater management went bust. I wish it hadn't, because I was the first to be sorry, the first casualty. But my part in what happened was so little that the dances and songs I was allowed to perform the way I liked in the revue went down very well in all the other German cities where I performed afterward. I should also say that in Berlin itself, every night, the five scenes I appeared in got the most applause from the audience, who I'm sure only wanted one thing: to be able to applaud the whole revue in the same way, if only it had been good enough.

One month was enough to kill off that terrible show. But the management asked me, on faith, to extend my contract for seven days for one thousand marks a day.

I accepted.

On the first day of the extension, I was doing my makeup when, suddenly, Pepito came into my dressing room.

"Stop!" he shouted. "The manager has duped us once again. In this very theater, an operetta is opening—tomorrow. Our extension without a contract is a trap. Tidy up your makeup and costumes and let's get out of here."

No sooner said than done. We quickly stuffed my costumes into two bags. I didn't even stop to take off my makeup. We left with our bundles on our backs, got into a taxi. Goodbye, Westens.

Imagine what happened in the theater. The Berliner audience was waiting, getting impatient, complaining . . . Their murmurs soon became shouts. Their protests turned into a racket, a riot. Two hundred policemen were needed to clear the auditorium. They reimbursed tickets at random. Even the people on the guest list got their hands on twenty marks.

Back to Berlin . . . It's one of the most beautiful capitals in the world, the one that best manages everyday life. You won't find such polite policemen or such well-mannered workers anywhere else. I should add that in Berlin, like everywhere in Germany, hospitality was pushed to the strangest level of refinement. It was almost worrying. As for the women in Berlin, I was surprised by how elegant they were. It was undeniable; I saw it for myself: I would admire them at the cabaret I ran on Behrenstrasse—where there was no trouble.

In the west of Berlin was a new, rich city, welcoming, sparkling, joyful, with the Kurfürstendamm cutting through it. And the nightlife had an intensity and a diversity that even Paris didn't have. There were grand cafés and grand restaurants like gigantic ships. Orchestras everywhere, from top to bottom, making sweet and rhythmic sounds like machines.

Two things in Berlin were like a dream to me. The first, silent: the aquarium at the zoo. The second, deafening: the huge Vaterland, where every country in the world made their mark with their own specialities, restaurant and theater.

In Stuttgart: two weeks at the Friedrichsbau Theater, two weeks inside a delicious candy jar, two weeks of success. Thank you, Stuttgart.

It's a strange country, Germany.

In Leipzig I starred in a variety show at the Krystallpalast. A master of the music hall, a Frenchman, I think, exhibited an incredible collection of snakes, goats, and crocodiles.

Great work.

One day, what should arrive in my dressing room but—listen to this—three darling crocodiles goose-stepping along and wagging their tails behind them. I adore animals, but those three little crocodiles—and quite a healthy size, too—were looking at me as if . . . I must say I was scared . . . And then all three of them, those little sweethearts, started a tap dance with their teeth. They were applauding with their big, chomping mouths. Oh! No, thank you. You see, I still prefer mice, although mice can . . . Well, ask any lady, it's terrible.

The Krystallpalast was full every night, all two thousand five hundred seats, and I guarantee you that everyone enjoyed themselves.

Leipzig, the Leipzig Fair, a fair that was everywhere all the time, with palaces, warehouses, banners, and parks. A city of engines, books, and signs. The station, the biggest that's ever been built. Apart from that, the worst coffee in the whole of Europe, even at the Auerbachs Keller that Goethe made famous.

✦ ✦ ✦

"No, Mademoiselle, you will not dance in Munich."

"But . . ."

"Mademoiselle, Munich is a respectable city."

And so I didn't dance in Munich. The police didn't want me to.

"Munich is a *German* city, is it not?" I asked them.

Munich, it's true, is a jealous city, the oldest and most deceptively beautiful in Germany, proud of its Greek-style replicas, its army of churches, its enormous squares, its avenues that are as wide as anything; proud of that unique building, the Deutsches Museum, where all the inventions of humankind starting from the first man are displayed along twenty kilometers of perfectly lit galleries.

It was twenty-two degrees below zero. I was freezing under my furs—I had been expecting Munich's audiences to warm me up with their applause.

"No, Mademoiselle, you, yourself, are the very definition of immorality."

Munich's police force had spoken.

Munich: a sort of dethroned capital that didn't know which saint to devote itself to anymore. It was full of Americans and steamed food.

All the same, I do have good memories of Munich, because of my pastimes that let me get to know it better and because of the beer. Luckily, the police didn't ban me from drinking beer.

Finally, I'll tell you about Hamburg.

Hamburg was America for me, with good American cuisine—a little greasier and heavier, though.

Hamburg: my best memories of Germany.

Hansa-Theater: a model European music hall, an outstanding venue where everything happens in a split second. I went onstage very early. At ten thirty, I was in bed. Sleeping early, Monsieur Sauvage, what a joy!

That's where I sang the big hit "Ich Küsse Ihre Hand, Madame," "I Kiss Your Hand, Madam."

Munich may not have wanted to see or hear me, but Hamburg . . . What an extraordinary welcome. Thank you, Hamburg.

Plus, I saw a little elephant there who had just been born at the zoo. He was called August. He was hilarious.

I should mention Hagenbeck, naturally, but who doesn't already know about Hagenbeck and his animals? His magnificent wild animals in Hamburg. You know, I really believe that certain wild animals are the last true kings.

That reminds me: around the same time, I got a very tempting letter. I keep a collection of amusing letters like this one. Here, read this:

Mademoiselle Baker,

I know that you earn a lot of money. Would you like to earn more?
My name is Jean V . . . I lived in Africa for ten years; I was

a Goumier, the commander of a harka. I only ever saw one airplane cross the desert, and what a desert it is! I often encountered wild animals, of which there are still many in Africa. They are sold for their weight in gold.

I then returned to live with my mother and older sister in France: they own a large grocery in Bordeaux. I was unwell. This was seven years ago.

I am now thirty-four years old and I want to make a good living for myself. I am a businessman and I have the benefit of knowing Africa well.

I would like to make you a proposition. I have not spoken about it with anyone else because I know it will interest you. As you know, lions, panthers, and all the rest are sold for their weight in gold. I would like to collect as many of them as possible. The plan I have in mind is a good one. It requires men and money. I shall supply the men: a rather large army. I will place them around the Negro continent at intervals: along the Atlantic and Indian coasts as well as those of the Red Sea and the Mediterranean Sea, forming a ring. They will set off when I give the word, gradually closing in on the Great Lakes inland. They will drive all the animals toward the center of Africa. As the circle shrinks, I will dismiss the men and the costs will diminish. Finally, all the animals will be in place. All that will remain is to take them, and we will sell them in Germany and America. A standard lion can sell for twenty-five thousand francs, even thirty. I know all the best places, but I am lacking some money. What do you think? I will send you an estimate, but tell me by return post how much you can provide. You will not regret it. I should add *that we will do everything by the book. In any case, I will need more than one hundred thousand francs. Please do reply. I will await your orders and I send you, Mademoiselle, my best regards.*

Sincerely yours,
JEAN V . . .

P.S.—If you do not accept, I know who else to talk to . . .

I should have given this letter to Hagenbeck in Hamburg.

But Hamburg—there is an astonishing cabaret quarter—its port is also called Hamburg. Endless quays; with all the skinny black arms of cranes and masts next to each other, it's like an immense forest of metal and deadwood, not a green leaf in sight if it weren't for the pavilions. I watched the big boats set off.

My European tour was over.

And I had to leave, too, leave soon for the South, across the ocean, toward Argentina and Brazil.

Argentina

Spring 1929.

Sunshine over the whole of Italy, a country of white and blue: snow, marble, and sky.

And avalanches of flowers.

Genoa is a little port town but a very important one. An old lighthouse at the base of a ring of silver hills and lavish villas. A thousand black barges in the shadows of tall ships. San Giorgio looks out to sea: it's a checkerboard that rises over the old arcades where sailors buy food and drink. A checkerboard that shrinks in the distance until it's just a tiny checkerboard . . . The *Conte Verde* reached the open sea, and its slow propeller made the sky-blue water bubble behind it.

I watched Italy from the highest gangway on the ship, watched Europe, which would soon be nothing more than a thread on the horizon behind us. A thread upon which the setting sun looked like a teetering tightrope walker.

✦ ✦ ✦

The sun fell over the other side of Europe.

A sea smooth as oil.

Stars above and below.

Fourteen days between the sea and the sky, the longest sea crossing of my life. But a fun journey. Deck chairs, the sea breeze, the captain, lunches, dinners, white birds playing hide-and-seek in the clouds. The ocean had its own clouds in the water, too, its own shades of color, fantasies of clouds inside. Parties, the wireless, phonographs. Cocktails and secrets at the bar.

I imagined America dancing toward us little by little. But first they told us we had come face-to-face with the equator and that it was time, of course, for the traditional crossing-the-line ceremony, the fancy-dress ball . . .

"The first prize for ugliness," said the steward, "goes to Mademoiselle Josephine Baker!"

I had dressed up as a very fat nanny.

We moved slowly past Rio de Janeiro without stopping, a dreamland of palms and shades of white before our eyes. We had reached America—at least by sight. We obediently followed the contour of the coast south and then, in the glory of the midday sun, there was Buenos Aires, the biggest and most modern city in South America. A city of squares—a game of cubes—each one a hundred meters squared.

I can really say my impresario gave me superb publicity there. And the city gave me its own publicity, too, on just as grand a scale—but dreadful. Just like in Central Europe, I was damned, a scandal, a femme fatale, a horrifying demon who lived off human hearts and ground glass. They even said I ate live rabbits and kept their bloody feet as lucky charms. And that's not all—but people won't believe me, and I don't want to hurt those Argentinians who push their morality and nationalism as far as . . . that far.

Anyway!

It was, clearly, a particularly difficult beginning. President Yrigoyen—you know what President Yrigoyen's career was like—thought the dancers in *Aida* were unbearable. As for me, he thought I was the shame of humanity. And so, without having any say, I once again became part of a truly violent political battle. President Yrigoyen seethed about me in the *Calle*, the biggest newspaper in Argentina at the time. My supporters—I didn't know them any better than I knew my opponents—responded with long articles in the *Crítica*. They would fight, almost slit each other's throats at the theater doors. The police called in whole armies of officers, to no avail. There was close combat between the salesmen of the two rival newspapers. My honor guard was made of *Crítica* street vendors. I must say, however, that the South American journalists generally acted impeccably toward me . . . President Yrigoyen, who devoted such odd articles to me, was not a journalist.

Despite, or maybe thanks to, this, the theater was full every night. Fittingly, on the night of the fiftieth performance, Monsieur Yrigoyen's supporters organized a demonstration. Inside the theater, all hell had broken loose: people were shouting "Down with Yrigoyen!" and lighting firecrackers under the seats, barrages of firecrackers that flew around the room.

Some women fainted.

The men punched each other.

We nervously lifted the curtain and dropped it back very quickly. The shouts got even louder than before: "Long live Yrigoyen!," "Down with Yrigoyen!"

I, personally, didn't want to leave the stage. Demonstrations have never scared me. On the contrary. And the musicians in the orchestra, hunched over, were furiously playing all the tangos in their repertoire.

On the night of the two-hundredth performance, Monsieur Sauvage, the theater, which could hold two thousand five hundred people, was still full. The impresario was celebrating while still shaking. A charming impresario. "I've never earned as much money," he said, "as with Miss Baker . . ."

I would have liked him to thank President Yrigoyen, but he always refused to do it. That was a mistake.

I left Buenos Aires in turmoil and took the train to continue my tour of Argentina.

First, I performed in Rosario, which really smells like wheat because all the wheat in Argentina piles up there, on the docks. Liquid wheat like honey, leaking from sacks, trains, and machines.

Next, it was Córdoba, a nice Catholic city where they welcomed me without a fuss. One of the local residents even gave me a gift, very courteously: a newborn cougar. I had never had a newborn cougar before! Sadly, he died . . . I was heartbroken.

Next . . . Next, I went back to Buenos Aires.

Everything had calmed down.

I danced in four different places there: the Astral, Fenix, Empire, and Florida cinemas. The president of the Alliance Française, Monsieur Saint, threw a party in my honor. Monsieur Saint gave me three little crocodiles—that is my best memory of Argentina, along with La Peña: the circle where all the artists came together, and it was run by a Frenchman. I'm always happy to see a Frenchman, whether I'm inside or outside France! You can always be sure he'll understand you and give you a warm welcome.

Did I already tell you what a magnificent city Buenos Aires is? Oh, the *paseos*! Palermo, Tigre . . . Buenos Aires, if you're interested, has the biggest brewery in the world. It also has the best tango orchestras. That's why I wanted to sing three tangos in Buenos Aires: "Mama Yo Quiero un Novio," "Garufa," and "Haragán." The titles don't mean much, but what tangos they are, like tender waves . . .

One day I was secretly taken to the suburbs of Buenos Aires.

There, they showed me how to cook an entire cow on a charcoal fire. A very kind man came with a knife that looked like a sword and cut a steak for me, straight from the cow, big enough to feed an ogre . . . It spoiled my appetite completely. I was very sorry. I would have liked to try and eat the whole cow to make him happy, that man.

Uruguay

The countries of South America are still only countries for show: a few big ports, a few very beautiful capital cities in beautiful surroundings, but behind these things are regions that are little known or even unknown. Some completely unexplored: swamps, deserts, untouched forest, and adventure. But the height of civilization is this: when you arrive in Argentina, they immediately treat you as a suspect. Whoever you are, you have to take yourself to the detectives in the anthropometry department. It's a charming welcome . . . "Your fingerprints, please" . . . and they dip your fingers in black grease. After that, you can take part in any revolution you like, take a side in the tango debate. Is the tango from Argentina or Uruguay? That's the question . . .

All I know, personally, is that Uruguay is a beautiful and very sweet country.

Montevideo is on the banks of the Río de la Plata, on the other side to Buenos Aires, two hundred sunny and watery kilometers away.

Uruguay is proud of its soccer world champions, and Montevideo is the proud home of the tallest skyscraper in South America.

Uruguayans are much more welcoming, much more outgoing than Argentinians. I have the best memories of that place. No incidents, no scandals. Excellent journalists. The best-behaved audiences. And then, from high up in the *cazuela* . . . Well, I'll tell you about it in a moment.

In the houses by the port, I heard people talking about a mysterious region: Chaco, a land of Indians in the middle of America. To get there, you travel as far as you can up the Río de la Plata, which splits into two rivers: the Uruguay and the Paraná. It's a dream, they told me, to travel along the Paraná on old boats, through the mosquitos and crocodiles. I, personally, have never seen Indians despite my interest in getting to know them.

I would really have liked to see the ones who, instead of washing their faces in the morning, paint them! Apparently, the women have extraordinary decorative paintings on their foreheads, their cheeks, and their necks, drawings of flowers and animals. When their husbands kiss them, they're kissing landscapes or still lifes at the same time.

When you travel on horseback, an Indian will travel on foot. He'll arrive long before you.

Some of them also go crazy for honey. They climb the trees like squirrels.

At night, in some areas, salt oozes out of the ground. Tapirs sneak along to lick the salt off the ground, but the Indians lie in wait to kill them. They stab them with spears.

The Indians are at home in Chaco, as they always have been.

They completely remove the hair from their bodies because they don't want to look like animals.

When they are twenty years old they can eat an entire cow in a single night and without having to force themselves. Then they don't eat again for four days. They drink. But usually, they eat little more than *jacaré*—that's crocodile. Crocodile tripe, snakes' tails, and palm hearts, that's what they value in Chaco. And they dance every night to the sound of tom-toms and gourds filled with stones that you can hear from very far away, across the plains.

When an Indian dies, all the others leave the village to go and settle somewhere further away, where they can peacefully smoke their pipes and drink chicha—it's made of honey and cooked, fermented fruit. Indians paint their lips as a sign of mourning.

I heard about all this on the docks of Montevideo, which are piled up with mountains of animal skins, feathers, horns, tinned food, and bottles of Liebig.

I performed in the Urquiza Theater, a big, modern theater. But there, the women don't sit with the men. They have a big balcony all to themselves that runs around the auditorium: that's the *cazuela*. I don't know why, but it made me think of old Turkish harems.

Every day, from high up on the *cazuela*, the women would lean over and throw flowers at me, bouquets of violets, big, sweet-smelling violets.

Isn't that lovely? I was very touched. Since then, I've kept lots of those violets in my books; they've dried between the pages. My whole collection of Edgar Wallace detective novels is full of them. Crimes and violets, excuse the connection.

There was a festival for the children, so I gave out gifts and toys on every *cazuela* in Montevideo. I even became a prisoner: they didn't want me to leave. They made me take bouquets of flowers. I was loaded with so many I couldn't walk. I was perfumed by all the gardens in Montevideo.

In Montevideo, I met Count Keyserling, the philosopher who founded the School of Wisdom in Darmstadt. We visited Pocitos with him, a magnificent beach, the Cannes of Uruguay, where all the country's fortunes and finest figures collide. The sand there is golden. Count Keyserling was also with us for the return trip from Montevideo to Buenos Aires. We never talked about philosophy, of course, but in my memory book he wrote a page that I still treasure.

Chile and Brazil

An airplane full of Chilean journalists came to Argentina while I was performing in Mendoza. These men—who were very friendly, by the way—came to see the phenomenon that was Josephine.

They came as scouts.

They didn't find me unworthy of their country . . .

Chile is a ribbon of land running all along the west coast of South America.[10]

To get to Chile, you have to cross the Andes. First, we traveled through an area that looked astonishingly like Mexico. We wove between porcupine mountains—mountains lined with enormous cacti from top to bottom. Then the train turned, went up, down, and back up again. Suddenly, women were fainting in their carriages. We were at an altitude of three thousand two hundred meters. The air pressure dropped so much it made these women collapse, and the train staff had to run from one side of the train to the other carrying oxygen cylinders for them to suck on.

The train gave its passengers a good shaking, believe me. It made sure to look after the fainters as quickly as possible.

I looked out the train door. To the left, below the tracks, was an abyss filled with clouds; to the right, above us, was a smooth rock wall that disappeared into another layer of clouds. We were sandwiched.

We slapped the women's cheeks. We drank.

I saw an eagle there, just the one. It was going around in circles ahead of the wheezing locomotives. Its cry was sharper than any siren I have ever heard. Needless to say, it's not always possible to cross the Andes. Sometimes, there are up to ten meters of snow on the tracks. But what a sight, Monsieur Sauvage! Silver and crystal snowcaps in the sun: giant snowcaps. The forests are black like a flood of Indian ink, blue like precious stones, and red, in the morning and evening, like a Red Indian party, like arrows going up to the sky, like the landscape is dancing . . .

It's a small journey, this crossing from Argentina to Chile, which cost a lot more than going from Europe to America.

There were maybe twenty thousand people waiting for me in Santiago, around the station. It reminded me of my chaotic arrivals in Central Europe, but I was a lot more worried. The stationmaster saved me. I ran across the tracks with him. He got hold of an old Ford like from a film and off we went! While the crowd called out for Josephine and broke all the windows in the neighborhood . . .

Sadly, the city of Santiago was flooded with little pieces of paper that said: "Warning, Catholics: Baker is here!" But the president of Chile, Monsieur Carlos Ibáñez del Campo, whom I am grateful to, explained to the mayor of Santiago—whose name I've forgotten— that you can't have good manners without being hospitable . . . So Santiago welcomed me warmly, and President Ibáñez was one of the first to come and see me at the Victoria Theater.

Santiago is a very beautiful European city that has President Ibáñez to thank for all its beauty, cleanliness, and liveliness. In fact, the whole of Chile should thank him for everything he did to make it as prosperous as it currently is. The Catholics really tried, a few times, to end my contracts, but the real triumph I had in the three theaters where I performed reduced them to silence.

From Santiago I went to Valparaíso, a city of white terraced houses that sit in the hills above the port. It's a sort of Monte Carlo, with hundreds of dazzling villas surrounded by shining greenery. They dance the cueca there, which is a sort of samba that I danced while everyone clapped and cheered.

Chile: my favorite country in South America. But I can assure you that Brazil is another beautiful, very beautiful country—the country of pineapples—with that unique wonder of the world: Rio de Janeiro.

When I arrived in São Paulo, the first Brazilian city I performed in—the railway line goes right between rows of banana trees—a lemon-yellow fire was dancing on the top floor of the Martinelli, one of the city's two skyscrapers. The other one is just opposite. They look like two big skittles, the pair of them.

São Paulo is an Italian city. Everyone speaks Italian almost all the time, and they're always talking about coffee, of course—although the "coffee kings" are nearly all in Rio de Janeiro.

Don't call Rio de Janeiro "magnificent"; it's much more beautiful than that: it's the paradise of Guanabara Bay. A bay perfumed by 364 little islands, all of them gardens, always full of flowers.

Rio is South America's City of Light. Every evening it becomes a wonderland that sparkles and reflects off the water. The suburbs are deep, rippling forests, full of strange orchids and mischievous monkeys. Hundreds of species of orchids. Thousands of monkeys playing around.

You must look at Rio from the top of the Sugarloaf, the mountain where you can enjoy the famous view. I wanted to see it from even higher, get a better view. So the city gave me an airplane—it was delightful.

Oh, imagine the films we could make there! My dream since then has been to make a film in Rio de Janeiro, the capital of colored people.

If you go to Rio, I recommend the *feijoada completa* with *farinha*—it's a dish of black beans with charred bread, dried meat, sausages, and smoked pork, another wonder, which you should wash down with a brandy they call all sorts of things: *cachaça, paraty, caninha* . . . So you can digest the meal properly.

You know, it was a Frenchman, Monsieur Agache, who designed Rio's layout.

I was at the Beira Mar casino, one of those promenades only to be found in Rio. There are other leafy promenades by the sea, too: Leme, Tijuca, Botafogo . . . When they want to build a promenade, they don't think twice about removing and carting off an entire hillside if it's in the way.

To perform in Rio, I first had to perform in front of the police and a censorship board. My first success.

In Brazil, I had nothing but success. But let's not say any more about that, please.

Let's talk about Brazil, the land of bananas and coffee. The gold bananas are smaller but tastier than the silver bananas. There are just as many types of bananas as we have types of pears in Europe.

Rio's beach, the prettiest and richest in the world, is Copacabana. Impossible to describe. But what I can tell you is that the sidewalks, like elsewhere in Rio, are made of multicolored mosaics, and at night, when there are people dancing the machicha everywhere under the lights, you'll think you're dreaming. I still can't stop myself from dreaming about it every night, when I listen to Carlito and his "boys" here in Paris—they were brought over by Madame Rasimi.

Let's not forget that Rio is a business city, but we can only criticize it for one thing: its single, idiotic skyscraper.

Oh, I almost forgot! I didn't tell you about the snakes. Brazil is also full of snakes of all sorts. I went to a snake farm near São Paulo. They seem happy there, tying themselves in knots, making their bodies into the number three, or eight, or question marks, living in big parks in sorts of tanks made of reinforced concrete.

Most of them were rattlesnakes. They are kept in Brazil to make vaccines and serums . . . And when I say "kept," that means not feeding them, because that's what you do if you want to collect lots of poison, good poison. Apparently, when snakes don't eat, they make poison. They store it in their hollow tooth. When the hollow tooth seems to be full, you squeeze the snake's neck and make all the poison come out the end, like a little fountain.

When a snake bites you, there's nothing to worry about if you bleed, or not much. Otherwise, it means that it's injected lots of poison into you, so you have to get help.

People usually don't like snakes, but I like them.

Rio de Janeiro. Oh, Rio! The *Lutetia*, the French ship, was already in the port, whistling, calling me. I went aboard, not without some regret but also secretly happy and a little afraid: I was going to see Paris again, I was going to try my luck in Paris again.

Ah yes, Monsieur Le Corbusier . . .

Monsieur Le Corbusier had been giving talks in Brazil. We became friends. I sang him little songs, he talked to me about architecture. We also talked about the botanical gardens in Rio— also impossible to describe. For the crossing of the line, he dressed up as Josephine Baker . . . If he hadn't been a famous architect, Monsieur Le Corbusier would have made an excellent music hall comedian. He could have done improvisation, would have been a great partner . . . Never mind.

And the *Lutetia* went on its way, on the calm sea that did nothing more than change color. In the mornings, I would watch its wake disappear in the distance while I sank my teeth into a fresh pineapple: there's nothing better for your health. I brought back a generous supply of pineapples and coffee, too. Imagine, I bought crates of coffee for three francs per kilo! But I'd forgotten about one thing: customs. My little coffee-importing plan was a disaster . . . My lovely Brazilian coffee cost me fifty francs per kilo in the end.

And that's how my first theater tours ended, my first adventures.

I had left Paris. I was returning to Paris. I wanted my biggest success to be in Paris and to have a house in France.

4

A CINEMATIC TURN

Cinema these days is Negro art, too: images, dancing, sun, blackest night.

Later on I'll go to the cinema every day. I'll have a cinema in my house. No telephone, no wireless—what a bore, that telephone! You talk, and I can't see you. I'd rather see you and not hear you.

Each country flashes before your eyes. I filmed with Monsieur Nalpas for the Folies revue. They'd set up light machines in Passage Saulnier. I looked straight into the lights, Nalpas told me I shouldn't. The little girls were shouting. I, personally, am not scared of getting sunburn in my eyes. I would shoot films that were written for me, starting with a screenplay written by Monsieur Maurice Dekobra.

A gentleman came. Where from? How? And who was he? I had absolutely no idea. A gentleman. You know, that mysterious character who's everywhere, behind every door, silently watching, slipping backstage like a shadow into the artists' dressing rooms; whom you happen to meet at every crossroad, behind a taxi, in restaurants; at the grocer's, the cinema, the hairdresser's, the candy seller, and even behind baskets of begonias in the city squares. The Fixer, Mr. Fix-it. A gentleman who has every man hanging off his right arm and every woman hanging off his left. A man with all the keys, all the tricks, and a smile.

So, a man came—a Russian, I think—who knew Monsieur Dekobra very well.

Monsieur Dekobra is a charming man who could—who wanted to—write a screenplay, a magnificent one, of course, a unique screenplay.

I was such a child! Such a fool yet so confident. I have changed a little since then. Dear me! But I don't like Monsieur Dekobra any less for it; he wasn't responsible, of course.

I learned to speak French and also to understand the fixers in nearly every language of the world.

Tell me, Monsieur Sauvage, can you swim?

Yes? Well! What if you couldn't swim and someone said, "Go on, jump in the water"?

Well! With me, you see, I threw myself in the water. I didn't know anything. I had absolutely no training in cinematography. I fell into cinema without a clue, *comme une fleur*, like they say here. Actually, I was quietly pushed, like this. And then: "You're on your own, Mademoiselle." I had what you might call "a name that sold well." That's always a good life preserver. Not one director thought to give me the basics; not one thought to help me, to teach me what I didn't know, what you should know before you start filming. So I swam . . . And by that I mean I couldn't; I didn't know how.

If I had to go to a cinema court today for what I filmed, I have no doubt that I'd be found guilty—but also, first and foremost, irresponsible.

Put this together however you want, it's all true, but be nice for everyone's sake, Monsieur Sauvage. So what? Sometimes there's a high price to pay for experience. I know that now. I don't ever want to dance, sing, perform, or shoot just because of my name.

I'm sorry. Let's carry on.

Actually, let's start again.

I shot three or four films: *Siren of the Tropics*, *Zouzou*, and *Princess Tam Tam*. Let's not talk about them for now. But next I do want to tell you why and how I love cinema.

I was brought up, Monsieur Sauvage, on graveyard stories.

A colored childhood is always a little sad.

Why have graveyards so obsessed colored men and women?

It happens in the moonlight, pale, pale as the screen; stones—marble lids—slowly turn over, and shadows come out of the boxes in the ground and unfold in all directions. Shades of people who, perhaps, during their lives, when they were actually alive, didn't do everything they needed, everything they would have wanted to do, who are trying again in the moonlight . . .

The first shades.

My childhood memories are full of these first shades. I used to be scared of them. I'm still scared of them, and yet I love them.

Other shades came after those ones, this time born of my fear or, rather, my love for fear itself. You know what I like to read? History books, collections of myths, crime novels.

Oh! Crime novels are real novels, much more than historical novels and much better than them, too. They're the only ones for me! I read them at night before going to sleep, on purpose.

Don't you think, Monsieur Sauvage, that the faded light in dreams is like moonlight or the light from a screen? Like a cinema in your head, shut away in the dark with the craziest, most beautiful, most bizarre, most warped images that symbolize things we should be able to understand, wouldn't you say?

I wake up suddenly in the middle of the night. The shades are there, they've all come out, the ones from my childhood and the ones from the books and the strange ones from my dreams. I get up. I tiptoe forward. I chase the shades and they disappear, melt in the light, in the bedrooms, in the bathroom, through the wardrobes, from step to step on the stairs, under the beds, among the curtains . . . Now all that's left is the house, lit up from top to bottom, like a screen where shadows have just been parading along, like an auditorium where the string lights have just turned back on after the show.

From there to cinema, it's only a step. Now you understand why I love—why I adore—the cinema. It's free play for all the sad or funny shades, a dream in black and white.

I've never seen beautiful, pure colors, the way I like them, at the cinema.

As a child, I'd go to the cinema to mix together the cheerful shades I was looking at with the gloomier ones from my memory.

To enrich my collection of shades.

Have you seen how I call, how I point to my foot with my finger? That's how I call up a shade, a memory, so I can perform. Everything within us must obey our fingers and eyes, wouldn't you say? Nothing must be ignored. Everything must be allowed to mean something. Unfortunately, these days, we've got used to only two or three simple, standard glances. We get stuck, we go stiff. Poor bodies, poor faces. Why don't we wiggle our noses, our ears, our toes? Our eyes are made to roll around, our muscles are made to work in every direction. And our faces: are they masks? Yes, these days they're masks. Unfortunately. Lifeless, dreadful masks. We don't dare laugh, or cry, or make funny faces. I make funny faces. I like it. It helps express things we can't express any other way, things we didn't know we knew. But tell me, who really knows, properly knows, the language of funny faces? From up onstage, I often look at the thousands and thousands of faces in the audience all squashed together and I think to myself, "Your job is to make these poor, unfortunate faces move, to change them, bring them to life. Voilà."

A little gymnastics, let's see.

Making different shadows play across my face as if on a screen.

A dark shadow that doesn't change, in a hollow in the face; it looks like a patch of ground to me already. So I think back to those old graveyard stories from my childhood and eventually I've had enough of them . . . Enough!

I love cinema, you see. How the images dance.

A film is a ballet—but *not* like a ballet on a music hall stage; hence, I think, the mistake we made in filming entire music hall revues without changing anything. And the pace? What happened to the pace? The pace isn't the same in a film.

The pace in cinema catches my attention and keeps me watching. I prefer it to all others because it's really up-to-the-minute, when it's real cinema. It doesn't always happen, though, and even less since films started talking, don't you think? You'd think they were talking ghosts. With those booming voices, my friend! Now all the cinema ghosts have become ridiculous, thanks to the 100 percent all-talking picture.

I went to the cinema in every country I visited. In every one, I wanted to see all the big films everyone was talking about. That— and my first plunge into film—will help me in the future because my greatest wish is to star in a big film, a beautiful and true one. Because for me, you know, cinema is natural, it's the whole truth and nothing but the truth, like we say to the judge, don't you think?

Well, I filmed *Siren of the Tropics* without reading the screenplay. No one cared or was considerate enough to have it translated into English for me. Why bother, right? Besides, this famous screenplay was only put together during the shoot . . .

But before that, before *Siren,* I filmed something else. Now,

Monsieur Sauvage, it was even more extraordinary, even more incredible . . .

During the Charleston days!

It already seems so long ago, don't you think?

That really makes me sad.

An old dance is more tragic than an old rose, an old, withered flower.

La Folie du Jour . . .

That was the name of the revue at the Folies Bergère, and it described the Charleston, too.

"Would you like to record the Charleston on film, Mademoiselle?"

"Why, yes, sir."

As we know, history—or legend—likes to think I singlehandedly imported the Charleston to France and Europe. Look at everything they wrote about it: I guarantee you'll laugh your head off for two hours.

The Charleston: a damned and tragic dance.

The line is destroyed.

The quadrille is dead.

The end of childhood.

Black witchcraft, the American convulsion, the end of the West . . .

Back to the point: I danced the Charleston in front of a cameraman. Oh! It was like a private party, a little family party. The same steps, the same makeup, the same . . . "frills." And what was the result? A dreadful thing—and no one, of course, to give me advice. I performed blind.

Angles and makeup: they're what really count, though. Adapting your makeup to the look of a scene, a performance, an atmosphere.

The originality, the character, of the makeup.

You have to emphasize the truth in theater, exaggerate the truth just to remain true, to preserve the truth, even—just as in music hall and in cinema. And every genre has its own angle just as it has its own pace, its own possibilities and limits.

Adapting . . .

You've got to have the gift of adapting.

Success is, first and foremost, about adapting—at least for those of us who are just interpreters. Artists who live off one trick that they use and repeat all the time, I don't like them at all. Artists that only have one face, one way of moving, one expression, they're machines. Then again, we're all under the orders of a machine, Monsieur Sauvage, and that machine is: stoo-pidity.

After my dancing debut in the cinema—in a very short scene—I filmed an entire revue: the Folies revue.

The year was 1926.

My second try was no better than the first. The memory is just as painful, but I would quite enjoy watching it again. What an important lesson! The main thing is to know what one shouldn't do again.

Oh, but wait! I almost forgot about something that didn't work out but which promised to be interesting and fun nonetheless. Joe Alex—a colored dancer, singer, and actor, who was one of my partners and whom I must thank, actually, for very cleverly making me practice my French songs and many other pieces—he had, before anyone else, suggested the idea of making a film with me . . .

Joe had even planned to set up a special company, a business, an enterprise, for colored artists living in France.

"What do you think?" he asked me.

"I like that!" I told him.

And we talked for many weeks about "Noir Film," its goals, its resources, its future . . . We kept talking . . .

And then we didn't talk about it anymore. It's a shame, because in France, in Paris, there are many colored artists who are great artists and even great French citizens. Unfortunately, people don't want to or don't know how to make use of them.

A studio . . .

A spotlight . . .

We're filming, my first time.

Cinema at that time was blinding. Where were you supposed to put your eyes? Mine were dry. Burning. My eyelashes and eyebrows were sizzling. I had no makeup on, no oil on my eyelids. I was blinded. Eyes are like hands when you're shy and you don't know where to put them, how to hide them. I couldn't see anything. I was in the middle of a fire; everything was burning under the harsh beams of the spotlights.

"Come on, Josephine . . ."

"If you will, Mademoiselle . . ."

On the other side of the fire, past the circular foyer, in the dark, in the night as deep as a hole, voices were speaking, giving orders, shouting . . .

I tried to look at the shadowy men but the jealous spotlights stopped me straightaway.

My first memories . . .

Prisoner in a magic circle . . .

Oh, that cameraman!

"Cut. Start again."

"Mademoiselle, stop looking at the camera."

I couldn't look at anything anymore. We stopped everything. My eyelids wouldn't even close. I was in pain for days and days.

Another time—later, much later, when there was absolutely no concern for common sense. In *Siren*, I ended up performing in the tropics in a fur coat.

So many bad decisions. Nothing but bad decisions! They didn't understand anything, anything at all about who I was. There was no attempt to understand, to make use of my skills. Forgive me for speaking so clumsily and a little bitterly. I hate things that are badly done, that could have been, and could be, done better—done *well*. These days, it seems everyone does a little of everything, however they like . . . Oh! All that wasted film tape. Does a director worthy of the name have the right to sacrifice art for money? You see what we've come to.

I was talking about things being unrealistic, about trickery.

In the ravines of my supposed wild Antilles, everyone could recognize, *did* recognize, the good old rocks of Fontainebleau, just outside Paris. Is that right? Poor Siren. But I would like to say a little friendly hello to the gorges of Blanchon and Barbizon, where I had a lovely time away from the cameras.

Beautiful landscapes.

What's the point of disguising them, tampering with them? They always show through in films, even when they're made to act as a different landscape, north or south. They're background extras who refuse to fool anyone . . .

Landscapes are honest.

Landscapes aren't set pieces; they're actors, too.

So, I was Papitou in *Siren*: at the Natan studio on Rue Francoeur, and at Théâtre Mogador, and in the middle of a Negro village in Épinay, and in Fontainebleau, and in the Hague.

The studio was made into the lobby of a travel agency. Papitou—the Siren of the Tropics—wants to leave her island to teach the Europeans a new dance. But she has no money! She miserably turns out the pockets of her hodgepodge of a dress; then she offers a talisman to the employee at the counter, but railway companies don't accept lucky charms. And they're wrong not to, because disaster isn't far behind. So the Siren hides in a corner and feels sorry for herself. Will she stay on her island? After a whole lot of trouble, she manages to get on a ship. But her mischievous sense of humor guarantees many more adventures on board. She tumbles down the hold and comes out all blackened with coal—I was tanned. Then she dives into an enormous chest and pops out covered in flour—I was white. A terrified old Englishwoman thinks she's a ghost . . . I saw ghosts of all colors, and they saw me in all colors in this film.

Tell me, Monsieur Sauvage: why, when a film is being shot, do film journalists feel the need to write little stories that are full of nothing, that have nothing useful to say, that are not true and are really rather silly? Why give words to something that is so far from having any? The "news" stories that were published while I was filming *Siren* sometimes upset me and made me laugh a lot: stupid things always end up being funny. Here, look at this little masterpiece; you should read it:

A fat lady, still out of breath from having climbed the seventy-eight steps separating the studio from solid ground, and stumbling right into the middle of the production without fully realizing what is going on, speaks to the colored star, who seems to be daydreaming beside a flat.

"What are you filming today, Mademoiselle?"

To this, Josephine replies in charming, mistake-filled French:

"Today *La Sirène des trois piqués*."

"The three *piqués*, the three crazies? I can surely see two," says the fat lady, pointing to two cast members who are fooling around in front of the beautiful star, "but where ever is the third?"

To this, Josephine replies, pointing to a fire officer:

"He there, but he not crazy he . . . lazy! A lazy fireman!"

Oh, no, no! Now that was just too awful—in a French newspaper, and a respectable one at that. It was a disaster, that story. Don't you think there's an obsession with this kind of gossip, like there's already an obsession with printed paper? We spoil everything . . .

I'm thrifty but at the same time I hate stinginess. I despise money. A director whose only concern is saving money is an awful director. Trust me, I know. But certain films that I shot—you can't imagine in what conditions!—some "made" quite a lot of money, as they say, however I, personally, hardly earned anything.

Not that it matters; it doesn't, I swear. And if the films had been good, I'd have willingly given up my pay . . . If only!

But let's get back to the point. I have lots of other memories: "In her hut, in the shade of the banana leaves, the Siren dozes in a hammock that is slowly swaying. The cameramen count the turns: thirty-four, thirty-five, thirty-six, thirty-seven, thirty-eight . . ."

All of a sudden, we hear a shout.

Another accident.

I have memories of being the first-aider on location and in the studio. One minute Georges Melchior was limping, the other Pierre Batcheff was tumbling down the rocks. I like looking after people. The women I admire the most in the world are the Sisters of Charity.

We were talking about Georges Melchior. He was so handsome and impressive in *L'Atlantide*! I remember how astonished I was, how happy, when during the last scene of *Siren*, I saw he had tears in his eyes while he was watching me perform. He had understood what I was capable of. Unfortunately, it was too late, and nobody around us was good enough, except Kranine, Alex, and his dog.[11]

We filmed a big scene at the Mogador under the heat of six monstrous spotlights. They made me wear a salmon-pink leotard with silver sequins.

It was loose, too long . . . The audience was full to bursting with well-meaning spectators and "critics," whose somewhat skeptical attitude I could sense even as I was dancing. So, bam, I tore off the bottom of my leotard in the middle of the scene, called over my dresser, and asked her to fix my accessories.

"Then we'll continue . . ."

Imagine the astonishment in the room—and how happy some of the spectators were.

They transformed the Éclair studios, in Épinay, into a Negro village. From our places under huts made of beautiful, brand-new yellow straw, we watched princesses and marchionesses merrily making their way to the guillotine . . . They were filming *Madame Récamier* next door. We were odd neighbors, to say the least. Negroes and sansculottes became drinking companions in a corner of the studio. This made Monsieur Barre, administrator of the Établissements Louis Aubert film company, say: "See? The Niger's not as far from the Seine as they say . . ."

And I danced the Charleston while they held their executions.

What's funny in cinema is when you get to hop from one set to another. Over here, the Negro village of Épinay; over there, as a very imaginative journalist said, "a large modern-style drawing room whose splendor is reminiscent of an Assyrian temple at the time of Semiramis and an ultra-fantastical nightclub with a suspension bridge holding a jazz band and around which stylized palm trees stand, interspersed with stuffed monkeys, true masterpieces of eclecticism and luxury."

You get the idea, Monsieur Sauvage. Then he wrote that it was "an orgy as Parisian as it is tropical."

I'd happily talk more about ugliness and camera appeal. It's something I've often thought about—something we don't think about enough, in fact, but I've already spoken so much about the art of making faces that we'll move on, shall we, it's all right . . .

While they were showing my latest film in Budapest, they asked me to come and perform in the intermission. So I stood in front of the screen, and whom did I see in a box to my right? Mistinguett! You know how much I admire and respect her— such a magnificent artist. So I immediately pointed her out to the audience and the journalists.

I said: "How did you not realize that the darling of Paris is with us tonight? Please, let's shout together: Vive Mistinguett! Vive Paris!"

I knew just enough Hungarian for that. And we brought the house down with applause. Everyone shouted, "Vive Mistinguett! Vive Paris!" and "Ra, ra, ra," three times, like you're supposed to, and "Vive la Hongrie!" three times, too. Mistinguett was very touched, I think. I'd brought her some flowers, and she threw them into the audience. What a wonderful audience!

✦ ✦ ✦

Cinema taught me what a Negro is.

"One Negro here," Marc Allégret would shout. "A Negro over there . . . Bring that Negro closer . . . Fetch me the Negro . . ."

I looked around for the Negro. They explained what they meant . . . It was what they called the blackboard they wrote lines on.

At that time, I was shooting my first talking film, *Zouzou*. There were still a lot of things I didn't know.

For a long time I didn't believe in talkies, didn't think they had a future. I, personally, thought it was impossible to make those

shadows have entire, proper conversations, to sing and shout—
that no matter what you did, it would just sound like a dog's dinner. But in 1929 I was at a boxing match in Vienna, and they were
filming it. The audience was shouting. People were bellowing.
Everyone was swearing at each other. It was funny. How could I
begin to imagine that machines could not just record all these
sounds, but actually make them sound real again? And so, when
I was watching the film and realized I was listening to the same
shouts I'd heard during the match, I was astounded, excited, spell-
bound.

We filmed in the summer of 1934, from the month of June to
the month of August, in Paris and Toulon.

The story is very simple. Jean Gabin is my brother without
being my brother. I love him without realizing I love him. Jean, a
handsome sailor, only has eyes for Yvette Lebon. And Pierre Lar-
quey, our father, has money problems. It's a nice film, as you can
tell.

"You're made for comedy," they told me. "You couldn't play a
lady!" Well! I prefer being myself anyway, without compromising.
I decided I would just have fun. I'd play practical jokes. I'd cause
a ruckus . . . "You are the devil" . . . Anyway, my character gets a
job in a laundry, where I have to iron the underwear of Edith
Méra, a big music hall star. And later on I will replace her, you
see . . . When the right moment comes, I drop the iron and wrap
myself in someone else's petticoat. First the audience is astonished, then everyone rises up like a pie crust. My audience is
astounded. And I'm delighted, I'm a success—the way it has to be,
of course. Since I can't have love, I make a name for myself . . .
The Bird of the Isles . . . Music, dancing, lights, oh, là là!

You'd never guess how many tragedies can go into a comedy—even in cinema. Just like any other part of life.

Before we started filming, I had a lucky charm, a tiny little black dog I named Zouzou, all curly. He was never further away from me than my handbag. One evening, both disappeared. I was heartbroken. "I don't care about the handbag," I said to myself, "but I want my little dog back." Neither one came back. I supposed the thief liked animals. That made me feel a little better.

No lucky charm to start with.

But we filmed all the same. In one scene I'm walking arm in arm with my sailor when we come across a cage hanging in a shop window. What do I do? Naturally, I open the cage . . . Come on birds, come on, be free.

I wanted them to put real birds in the cage so they could really leave, fly away. I thought: "If we redo the scene three or four times, I'll have given just as many little animals their freedom."

It's extraordinary, Monsieur Sauvage: the birds didn't want to leave. Maybe they believed in cinema. They certainly didn't believe in their freedom anymore. They preferred their little seeds. They didn't care a jot about me, in their cage. They were hopping up and down on their perches. It made me sad. So I gave them a good shake: the cage, the birds, and their seeds.

The director, Marc Allégret, was tying himself in knots: "Carry on, please, carry on . . ."

Next, I was to give a poor dog some water in the middle of Rue Lepic. I was meant to open a water hydrant on the side of the street, let it run slowly, and watch the poor animal. A scene of compassion, you see? But the dog *was* thirsty—in real life. So I turned the hydrant on full blast; I was seeing stars. It was like a geyser, that water! It went right up to the first-floor windows. Everyone was soaked: the actors, the people watching. But the cameraman thought it was much better.

The cameraman's name was Michel Kelber. The dog's name was Biquet. Poor Biquet! He died while we were filming the last scenes. He was so young. His illness hadn't been an act after all.

"Almost there, Biquet! Then you won't have to pretend anymore. You can come to Le Vésinet, to my house. I'll look after you, I'll really spoil you."

He did his scene; he couldn't take it anymore. His little belly was like a bellows. He went to die in a corner of the studio. I hugged him and I cried . . . Poor Biquet!

We're performing, you know; we're playing around. But real life is always there, setting you straight—death, too, Monsieur Sauvage. The truth of life . . . Always there. It's tough.

Do you know why Jean Gabin is a great, great actor? Because he never forgets the truth about life and death. When he acts—with such passion, I saw it from up close—there's something so simple, so poignant, something I can't put my finger on, it's beyond natural . . . It's supernatural, that's it. He never forgets that he's just a man like everyone else. That's what sets him apart. He's sincere. And he's handsome, he always will be. He knows . . . He never forgets. But sometimes he forgets himself. Anyway, he's marvelous.

If only you saw how he gave my Julot what for. I'm not kidding, I'm serious. We were at a dance.

Teddy Michaud played Julot, the "bad boy." He wanted me to dance with him; I didn't want to. I was supposed to take his hand and bite it. Meanwhile, Jean would beat him up . . . Okay, then! Jean showed up and bam, bam! That encouraged me. So instead of giving Teddy a nibble, I bit him until he bled. Then Jean started up again . . . We could have completely torn him apart between the two of us.

Unfortunately, Teddy Michaud—who was wondering what was going on; he thought we'd gone mad; the look on his face!—had to be taken to the infirmary and from there to the hospital to get bandaged up, our own colleague. He must remember that character, Zouzou.

An hour later, Jean Gabin nearly got arrested at the port in Toulon. And that was no joke, either.

After the incident with Teddy, Marc Allégret suspended the shoot. Jean was in his sailor's outfit—it suited him—and went for a drink in a café. A quartermaster went by with his patrol . . . Stop!

"You!" the quartermaster said. "You've been up to something. You should have been back on board half an hour ago. We're casting off in ten minutes."

Gabin laughed. But the quartermaster wasn't joking.

Fortunately, one of the officers who'd been assigned to work with us intervened:

"That's Monsieur Jean Gabin, the actor . . . Jean Gabin!"

The quartermaster looked confused.

"Why, just now," said the officer, "he gave one of his friends such a good going over that he had to be taken to hospital. I was there."

That's cinema for you. The real sailors were so happy that

they gave us a beret each, to Jean and me. Another lucky charm! It's not every day that a regular worker gives you a beret of honor. We put them through so much trouble, asking them to be extras.

While we were filming *Zouzou*, the producers published a newspaper, *Le Journal de Zouzou*, with a print run of six hundred copies. It was handed out all over France for publicity.

I learned, reading *Le Journal de Zouzou*, that my biggest dream was "to own a bed as large as that of Marie Antoinette."

That still amazes me. I know nothing about this bed of Marie Antoinette but it hasn't left my mind since. What could it be like?

Nothing but tall tales when you're making a film, even and especially when you refuse to become a "flashy" star. But none of that's important. The work speaks for itself.

Zouzou, an Arys-Roussillon production, with screenplay by G. Abatino—Pepito's brother—and dialogue by Carlo Rim, was a success. It was the breakthrough moment for Yvette Lebon and Viviane Romance. I was happy about that. It confirmed Jean Gabin's talent and why he is one of the greatest actors of our time. And me, I did my best.

In this film, the banana dancer left her bananas behind. I was the daughter of a showman. All actors and actresses are the children of showmen at heart. Without them we'd be nothing. I noticed that.

And the newspaper *L'Humanité* even wrote this about *Zouzou*: "the only music hall film directed in France that could compete with American productions."

What more could you ask for?

5

AN ENORMOUS APPETITE
AND SOFT SKIN

An Offering of Recipes

have an enormous appetite. My favorite food is a plate of spaghetti covered in red pepper. Italian spaghetti. I spend half an hour shaking the pepper pot over it. It's good. I know because I know how to cook. I often make dinner for my friends. I can make wonderful cakes.

"You'll realize later on," my mother used to say, "how useful it is to know how to cook."

She was right.

My specialities are: American stuffed buns, chicken with cream, fruit tarts, crepes with caviar, jellied rabbit, and Neapolitan-style macaroni.

I dare say that my crepes with caviar are the bee's knees.

But I never smoke and I don't drink, except beer. I went drinking a few times and I became so horrible . . .

I once had an extra-large American chef, a Negro: two meters tall with a white chef's hat and red eyes. He was just as cheerful as me, laughing from start to finish while at his grills.

His name was Freddy.

Hello, old Freddy!

Aren't we a funny pair, in our white aprons in the basement?

Here—in honor of Freddy, who loves food even more than me, here are four recipes you should try:

Beauharnais (or Creole) sweet potatoes

Peel the sweet potatoes and boil them in water with two grains of salt—no more.

Drain the sweet potatoes.

Next, mash them with a little salt, pepper, and butter (one small knob of butter for every three sweet potatoes).

Place it over the heat and stir quickly, quickly, while you add grated coconut: half a coconut. Pour in milk to make it creamy and beat it with a fork—don't be scared.

If you keep it thin, it's a soup. Thicker, and it's a sweet dish you can eat anytime, a sweet dish . . .

Hotcakes with syrup

Gradually mix together one pound of good flour, one tablespoon of baking powder—I don't know the French name for that powder—half a liter of milk, two whole eggs, and a tablespoon of good-quality melted butter. Add a little salt. Mix everything well and use a small ladle to pour it onto a hot plate greased with bacon fat or lard. Brown on both sides.

You serve these cakes with syrup or jam and butter.

And you'll want more!

Corned beef hash with poached eggs

Mix together a can of corned beef hash with a finely chopped onion and three boiled potatoes. Mold them into the shape of small bread rolls. Brown them in a frying pan—don't fall asleep—and serve with a poached egg on top. You can also eat corned beef hash with English tomato sauce: tomato ketchup.

I like to eat it with very thick tomato sauce.

Josephine Baker's flan

Take three fresh eggs—fresh, not like Chinese eggs—and three spoons of caster sugar. Beat it well, with two spoons of regular flour or rice flour. Mix in half a liter of milk little by little, and flavor it with two little spoonfuls of kirsch. Now, to this cream, add three bananas cut into rounds and little pieces of lemon peel.

Then cook it in the oven, but not too hot, in a flan dish, of course, for twenty minutes. You can eat it three hours later, when it's cold. You're going to love my flan.

It's good, Monsieur Sauvage, to eat well to stay healthy. The simpler the better. Red meat, rare meat, grilled, barely seared, all juicy. Chew it well before you send it down to your stomach . . . We don't chew enough anymore. We just suck it up, devour it.

Health is the best kind of beauty. If there weren't so many unwell people who don't know they're unwell but keep pestering us, the world would be more beautiful.

You can take more of those things, the same little pills. It's not worth it.

I have no desire at all to let people use my name to sell rice powders or eaux de toilette or lipsticks or cosmetics or soaps.

Those chemical products in little jars are, in my opinion, not great. They make your skin flaky.

First, you should dance as much as possible and sweat a lot. You'll sleep like a log afterward. Sleep clears your eyes: that's all you need for your eyes.

Ladies, sleep naked under your sheets.

When you do your makeup, don't do it by halves. Makeup should be noticeable; otherwise it's just a trick for the sick.

The best eau de toilette is rainwater; it keeps forever. A woman who's concerned about her skin should have a cellar stocked high with bottles of rainwater, sky water, beauty water.

Scrub your arms every day with a hard horsehair brush; that's what arms like.

Naturally, take baths—with violet milk, for example—warm ones. A nice long steam bath every month.

You should try to swim every day. Animals that live on land will never be as elegant as fish.

When you're tired, wipe your face in the morning and evening with flaxseed water. Boil the flaxseed in water for a quarter of an hour: easy.

I find that lotions and pastes made with fruit are the best, the most natural. Cucumber ointment: wonderful.

Preparations

1. Orange juice mixed with cologne and boiled water, in thirds: a lotion to soften the skin.
2. Banana water, to get rid of wrinkles, if you have any: cut five or six bananas into rounds and soak them in alcohol. After six days, the alcohol will have gone down; top it up with boiled water. Leave it to rest, then filter it. Wash with it gently in the evening.
3. Mash some very ripe strawberries and apply them to your nose, your forehead, and your neck. Wait for it to dry. This will give you a rosy complexion.

If you don't have strawberries, use grapes; you'll have skin just like a grape: supple, smooth, and clear. The skin of fresh figs is wonderful for this, too, and it helps with irritation and little pimples.

Beauty isn't everything. Do you have any pains? A little rheumatism? Try this for a remedy. It's foolproof. Take a really fat rattlesnake. Then skin it—*alive.* Then peel off the fat in the same way you removed the skin. It's very easy; you could do it with your eyes closed. Knead the fat with your hands, then press it through a strainer. Rub a little of this in, and you'll have no more pain. But the snake must be skinned alive, you hear. And it's hard to find the right kind of snake in Europe. All the better for him, poor snake.

Here's something easier for something different.

Do you have heavy blood, a little thick? That's not good for women. You must make it thinner. Mama had an excellent recipe. Simply eat beet leaves cooked in lard. Preferably with a big slice of cornbread. Wonderful. You'll look visibly younger.

People wanted to pass me off as blacker than I am, but I don't care to be whiter or any darker.

The real wizards are hairdressers!

I've just written a love letter to the Great Wizard himself. How funny . . .

Why? I ask myself.

You don't understand! Oh, là là . . . I should have given him a big hug and kiss . . . I didn't dare.

Antoine is the Great Wizard . . . I arrived at Rue Cambon, my hair "dressed with caviar," as the journalists wrote, meaning my short kinky hair was slicked down over my head.

All I had to do was sit in a comfy armchair and close my eyes. My dog Phyllis and her husband, who's as fat as a hot water bottle, both of them were sleeping in my lap.

His hands waved around my head . . . Oh! Just like that old magic business in St. Louis! I was shaking, but Antoine is a good wizard. He talked. He was good at talking.

"Do not think of anything, Mademoiselle, do not do anything that is not harmonious," he said . . . What does that mean?

I'm thinking, Antoine, about my dances; my pirouettes, as you called them, my giraffe walk, my kangaroo walk, and when I look like, you know, a saxophone that's moving . . .

There are people who don't think that you can bring harmony to these dances, too. And that you've got to be brave and keep smiling in front of the brutal incomprehension of the applause or the wolf whistles.

Meanwhile, I sensed the Great Wizard standing above me with his stern, unreadable expression. Searching. Imagining. I could hardly feel his hands: they were lighter than a fairy's . . .

The dance lasted a long time, getting lighter and lighter. Antoine wasn't talking anymore . . . What had become of my short kinky hair? I really wanted to know but I'd promised not to look until the end, so I could enjoy the surprise of meeting this strange Josephine . . . I was almost scared.

A new face is a new soul, too, you know. A new role to play. Antoine really knows it. He doesn't give hairstyles randomly. He never styles two women the same way. He knows the power of a face. What a sad mouth, a cheerful smile, can achieve when it's paired with this hairstyle or that. Every woman is an inspiration. And he's an inspiration for each of us as well, while he sculpts our hair in front of the mirror, our faces, too.

In Japan, you know, they never act without a mask. It represents the character's spirit. I, personally, keep my face; my mask is the hairstyle Antoine gives me.

For every one of my concerts, every one of my sketches, I made sure I had a different hairstyle to fit my role. It's more important than a new dress to make sure I sing and act well.

Pretty women really understand that, those who use hairspray.

They know what to expect from the artifice that transforms them, that creates different versions of them to capture a man's heart. Because these gentlemen are fickle, their tastes aren't reliable. That's why women have to go through all these comedies, these tragedies, farces, stories, all these transformations to stay the same but always different, every season, every hour.

Finally, I dared to look . . .

Antoine had respected my slicked-back, dancer's hairstyle. But he had decorated it with glazed spirals, leaves, flowers . . . He'd created a whole garden around my head.

I felt too shy to throw my arms around him. That's why I sent him that love letter.

I hope he hasn't lost it. Since then, Antoine's set up a hairstyling factory in New York, Fifth Avenue. Several floors. Big batches of customers sitting under dryers. Hundreds of women at once.

The hair wizard . . .

Antoine, and other hairstylists, too.

Jean Clément, for example, gave me a triple bun. Three buns of hair on my head, one on top of the other. Who was I this time?

I mean it when I talk about wizardry.

I know there are some signs one must believe in, some that are lucky and some that aren't. I also know full well that one shouldn't listen to all the talk one hears about the future. But I, personally, wouldn't want to walk underneath a ladder, I'd regret it soon after. Whistling is not allowed in my dressing room. Whistling is dangerous. It brings bad luck. It's a snake, a sign of death.

Don't eat animal heads in order not to get headaches. Putting iron between your teeth cures a toothache. It's unlucky to put your right shoe on first. Giving a knife as a gift cuts the ties of friendship. You shouldn't cross knives, or forks, or walk on crossed straws. Everyone knows that. Moving a piece of burning wood is unlucky. Cinders are sacred. No needlework on Thursday and Saturday afternoons. A thread spun on a carnival day will be eaten by mice.

There's a ghost, a guardian, that has its feet on the ground and its head in the sky.

Most of all, one shouldn't run after money. It's, what do you call it . . . It's liquid, it flows, you can't hold water, can't take handfuls of liquid.

I have money. One hundred thousand francs; it's nothing at all. Worth much less than a smile from a friend.

Yes Sir, that's my baby.
Oui, Monsieur, cela est mon enfant.

No Sir, I don't mean maybe.
Non, Monsieur, pourquoi dites-vous peut-être?

When you translate these songs into French, they become silly.

SURVEY RESPONSE
WHAT DOES THE FUTURE HOLD FOR WOMEN?

To Mademoiselle,
I have no idea what the future holds for women and no more of an idea about the present. That's not important. But I hate frills, and I

love my freedom. In any case, businessmen don't forget that we are women—all men are businessmen—and these days there is an obsession with the bedroom.

And women never forget that they are women. They're taking advantage of it more and more. I, personally, hate loose women, particularly the ones who want to seem honest. Either I love someone or I don't. As for the future, there's still time to think about that but I hope we'll be able to live naked. There are only a few women, and very few men, who could live naked, show themselves naked. That's all.

HOW I BECAME A SINGER

From Rue Pigalle to the
Club des Champs-Élysées, and Cabarets

n the past, after the show, I would dance every night at the Abbaye de Thélème, or the Impérial, or the Milonga—though it wasn't easy to dance with my arms, or on all fours, or to dance with my knees between the tables, among all those midnight savages who'd devour you with their eyes. Once it hits midnight, everyone up in Montmartre goes wild.

I thought, "Why not open my own cabaret?" So I set up. I opened my own bistro—you do say bistro, right?—on December 14, 1926.

I've never had so much fun. I made jokes, I stroked the bald men's heads, I tweaked the beards of those who had beards. I'd see them in the day, these men; they weren't laughing so much then.

And I'd also make the fat ladies dance—it didn't always make them laugh, but it always made me laugh, for sure. Everyone dancing the Charleston, the samba, swing dancing: the waiters, the maître d's, the chef, the cashier, the bellhops, the goat, and the pig . . .

As for me, I'd dance and dance, I'd laugh, I'd be in fits of laughter. I'd pinch the nose of whoever was closest and pull their ears, their hair, tweak their beards, and there go the streamers, the balloons, and lights changing all night long . . .

I'd eat dinner at five in the morning.

Sometimes—on Sundays—I'd dance for eighteen hours a day.

White men are odd creatures.

When I used to dance at the Abbaye de Thélème, every night I'd come home—alone. That shows there's something extraordinary that white people still haven't understood.

At the Abbaye de Thélème, I caught pneumonia for the first time. Pneumonia is a dreadful black beast with spikes all over it. A terrible time; it shook me up like a coconut tree. Everyone lost hope, like I was already dead. I was alone in that, too.

Look at me when I dance in the middle of you—this is how we should dance, not onstage but in the middle of a circle of people clapping, a circle that shrinks, in a crowd of men and women, on the same level, in the same light, side by side.

But when I'm not dancing, when I'm unwell, you'd better leave me alone . . . *If you like Ukulele Lady* . . .

My first cabaret, by the name of Chez Joséphine, was on Rue Pigalle. I wasn't paid but I was fed. I discovered soufflés . . . Oh, là là! The soufflés I had, my dear . . . Cheese soufflé, mushroom soufflé, vanilla soufflé, chocolate soufflé, rum soufflé . . . They just about gave me indigestion but I don't regret it. I left a month later.

Pepito was in charge of a cabaret on Rue Fontaine. I felt at home there with the rag dolls, this tall, crossing their eyes like I do: Josephines sat on every table. I'd dance with Josephines in my arms.

I still danced in the afternoons but not on Rue Fontaine: at the Acacias tearoom, near the Place de l'Étoile on Rue des Acacias. It became a rather bawdy place, that tearoom. A place for American women who were passing through, and for gigolos, cute things with silk handkerchiefs in their breast pockets to wipe away lipstick.

I'd never have thought you could earn so much money from hot water. It's a whole business. We'd quickly dip a little teabag into four or five pots in a row, to give them some color. Oh! We'd leave it in the water for as little time as possible, that little teabag. Now it's different; you don't share teabags. Everyone wants to see one in their teapot. But that wasn't an option at Acacias. Dip, serve! Everyone was happy.

I wouldn't have dared sing in public at that time, either. But my friends on Rue Fontaine were determined to make me.

I would croon to myself at home, little bits of different songs: la la la, ti ti ti, while I played with the cat, nothing more.

"Josephine, give us a song!"

"Josephine, give us a song!"

"Josephine . . . !"

I thought they were going to break everything in the club, these men-about-town: the glasses, the ashtrays, the ice buckets.

Never mind . . .

I sang a little verse, but it didn't come out right; I choked on it. But day by day I got used to it. I started improvising . . . And that's how I became a singer.

"Pretty Little Baby": the first song I performed in public.

At that time, my pig had got so fat from eating all the leftovers in the cabaret kitchen that he'd struggle to get himself under the boiler where he used to sleep. His back was completely roasted, my little sweetie pie. And he'd graze himself so badly it bled. One evening he was in a foul mood and he lifted up the boiler, pipes and all. And he kept getting fatter—he couldn't fit through the kitchen door anymore. We had to knock down a section of the wall so he could get out. Poor pig! He was like a barrel that we were rolling along, with his soft ears mopping the floor.

Away from the cabaret, I was still just a "naked attraction," a silent one, at the Folies Bergère.

Monsieur Henri Varna, the artistic director at the Casino de Paris, is the one who saved me from all that shimmying. He gave me my place as a music hall star.

You can be friends with your directors in the theater. I always was, equally, with all of them. I couldn't work anywhere without making friends. But I'm very fond of Monsieur Varna, fonder than I am of any other friend. And his mother, my Lord! What a charming lady. I'm truly grateful to her because, before I started at the Casino, when people used to say all kinds of things about me—"Her body is fantastic, you can't argue with that, but it's not enough"—Monsieur Varna's mother kept saying: "This girl will be a big star one day, believe me."

And because Monsieur Varna was a good son, he hired me.

He taught me the tricks of the trade. I'm grateful to him for that. But even more grateful that he knew he needed to protect what gave me and other artists our character. He doesn't twist the things he'd like people to pay attention to. Monsieur Varna is a master of nuance, a tasteful and measured man. He let me do what I wanted onstage; guided me, too. He trusted me.

My first time onstage at the Casino, I was dazzled, shaking, lost. Then I heard the thunder of applause. I rushed forward. I was overwhelmed. I shouted: "Thank you, oh, thank you! Thank you very much, ladies and gentlemen."

"No, my darling," said Monsieur Varna. "You are not a street performer. Don't thank them like that. You're not at the cabaret. Look at me . . . Bow to the right, to the left, gracefully, with grandeur and kindness. You're the big star now."

But I'll say it again: the audience is my family. I throw myself into their arms. I love the audience, especially my Parisian audience. And they know full well when you're performing honestly. They love being loved.

With Monsieur Derval at the Folies—as we called it—it was always different. Monsieur Derval is the king of artistic directors. No one compares to him for strategy, even in America. I'm not just flattering him—I've spent time with enough American theater producers, believe me. His preparation is mathematical, down to the minute; his productions, even the craziest, most imaginative ones, are mathematical. Backstage is a laboratory. It's very efficient here; one is shown at one's very best by the sets.

The audience knows so little about what directors are like. They imagine them the wrong way. Monsieur Derval stands bolt upright, tall; he looks strong and gruff but he's sensitive, like a child. It's inevitable. A director without considerable, profound sensitivity wouldn't be in tune enough. He wouldn't otherwise be able to touch the audience—the biggest, most diverse and freest audience, the one you find in music halls.

Plus, Monsieur Derval has a one-of-a-kind wife: a blessing, so elegant, with her fabrics and colors and frills, the most exquisite costume designer. The most tireless. A tyrant with all her fittings. I hate fittings. Lift your arm. Bend down. Turn your head. One more pin, two pins; three, four pins; five, ten, thirty pins. My job isn't to be a pin cushion.

I stayed with my cabaret on Rue Fontaine for two years. Then I gave it to Jane Aubert, whom I deeply respect. She was a star long before me; I heard her at the Abbaye de Thélème. She made me feel hopeless, did Jane. She was so good, seemed so comfortable, at the cabaret.

Anyway, in 1937, during the Colonial Exposition, Chez Joséphine Baker could be found on Rue François 1er. It was a quiet spot, packed every night with faces from all corners of the earth who came to see the sights of Paris. They weren't thinking about the war yet. "Pretty Little Baby" is what I sang—or, more emotional, these lines, which I preferred:

Suppose . . .

Then war broke out.

Everything changed so much then. The joys that survived changed tone. Pleasure wasn't the same. It was less honest. You could say it was anxious. There was something forced about it. Sometimes nightclubs became snake pits. But they became more spectacular, I think, more diverse, more artistic. People didn't say "cabaret" anymore: the word shrunk in the wash with everything that happened. People said "club." "Let's go to the club!" They'd come to listen to Josephine at the Club des Champs-Élysées on Avenue Montaigne . . . Club 48, Club 49, the chic club. You'd go down a few steps. Walk between the pillars. I'd be pinned against a pillar by the lights, making my back cold. Singing as if to myself:

C'est à minuit que tout paraît surnaturel.
It's at midnight that everything seems supernatural.

I'd sing some more, between the white feathers of a big fan waving gently to finally chase away the bad memories:

Paris, Paris, Paris . . .
Madame, c'est votre robe si jolie.
Paris, Paris, Paris . . .

Paris, Paris, Paris . . .
Madam, it's your very pretty dress.
Paris, Paris, Paris . . .

At the club, Monsieur Spaak, the Belgian prime minister, asked me to come to his table. He's nice. The king and queen of Belgium were at the club, too; what an honor. They were in disguise. By that, I mean the whole room recognized them right away. The maître d's were uncomfortable. The florist didn't dare move. But the king and queen waved them over. They're very nice.

And Aly Khan with Rita Hayworth, near the orchestra—very, very nice. And Emperor Bao Dai, his hair just as black as mine, just as shiny and slicked back. Stopped still to listen to me. He was holding his matchbox so delicately, like it was a lump of sugar. Everything seemed delicate in his hands. Even the used match between his fingers seemed precious, while he was listening to me . . .

Mais oui, mais oui, pardi,
Ce que j'en dis on vous l'a déjà dit.
Mais c'est Paris . . .

But yes, but yes, of course,
I've told you what you already know.
But that's Paris . . .

7

FROM THE STAGE TO THE GRAMOPHONE

From Negro Songs to "Ave Maria"

love gramophones: I've tried all the brands in the world.

At first there were seven Odeon records that showed off my voice. Like them?

"Who?," "Dinah," "That Certain Feeling" . . .

That certain feeling the first time I met you
I hit the ceiling I could not forget you.

. . . "Sleepy Time Gal," "I Wonder Where My Baby Is Tonight" . . .

I burned up every letter
And thought that I'd feel better
. . . I wonder where my baby is tonight . . .

. . . "Bam Bam Bamy Shore," "I Want to Yodel," "You Are the Only One," "Feeling Kind of Blue," "Brown Eyes," "Always,"

"I Love My Baby"—I like those last two songs more than all the others:

> *Not for just an hour*
> *Not for just a day*
> *Not for just a year*
> *But always, always*

✦　✦　✦

If you want to know Negro songs—the real ones—you need to go down the Mississippi on one of those boats that are still pushed along by big paddle wheels.

It's nighttime, and the boat's big balance wheels are slowly turning, turning. The banks of the Mississippi pass by on each side: woods, farmland, prairies, and marshes where hot gases bubble up.

It's nighttime, and there are Negroes sitting like statues by the river, singing their songs, old slave songs, gentle, sensual, like chants—or others that are short and passionate, full of shouts, full of movements.

And they often sing old songs from Africa, from old Africa, without realizing it, like this one, for example, that a friend wrote down for me:

THE SONG OF AHAN

> *Hi-Ho-Mang' Moussa*
> *Sing, sing, paddler in front*
> *Hi-Ho-Mang' Moussa*

Hi-Ho-Mang' Moussa

Ho-Yo-Sa-Hi-Gan

Sing the great singers of the wind

Hi-Yo-Rott'-Sa-Hi-Gan

Ho-Mang' Moussa

Ho-Mang' Moussa

The great sorrow of the men on the water

Oh! The great sorrow

Of the black men

Of the black men

Of the black men on the water

Oh! The great joy of the workers of the water

Yo-Ho-Yo-Ho-Yo

Ho-Rott'-Ho-Sa-Hi-Gan

Lift the bar, lift the bar

Lift the bar, paddler

Ho-Mang' Moussa

Sing, paddler in front

Sing the workers of the water

Hi-Ho-Mang' Moussa

Hi-Ho-Mang' Moussa-Yo

Doesn't it remind you, Monsieur Sauvage, of Russian songs—the boatmen? Shame we don't have the music.

The Europeans would like to impose very strict rhythms onto these songs. They don't understand that there can't be rhythms other than the ones of that night: of chance, place, and blood.

Medicine songs . . . meant to relieve tiredness and grief, ease sadness and bitterness, comfort nightmares of the sun or moon, kill nerves and soothe burns inside or outside the body.

People don't know how to translate Negro songs. Simpler is always better. The same goes for American songs copied from Negro songs.

How should we translate them? Here . . . I'll try . . .

THE LAMENT OF MANAMA

Love came

Death came with love

The moon came with love

The moon is a thief

The moon took my pretty baby

Love is death upon death

The sun came

Love will not return

It's already six in the morning

Now work with your hands

. . . Work with your hands

. . . Work with your hands

UKULELE LADY

I saw the splendor of the moonlight

On Honolulu Bay

There's something tender in the moonlight

On Honolulu Bay

And all the beaches are filled with peaches
Who bring their ukes along
And in the glimmer of the moonlight
They love to sing this song
If you like Ukulele Lady
Ukulele Lady like a'you
If you like to linger where it's shady
Ukulele Lady linger, too

✦   ✦   ✦

J'ai vu la splendeur du clair de lune
Sur la baie d'Honolulu
Il y a quelque chose de si tendre
Au clair de lune
Sur la baie d'Honolulu
Sur toutes les plages de belles filles
Qui viennent avec leur gazouillis
Et dans la lumière très douce du clair de lune
Elles aiment à fredonner leurs chansons
Si vous aimez Madame Ukulélé
Et que Madame Ukulélé vous aime
Si vous aimez vous attarder dans l'ombre tiède
Madame Ukulélé s'attardera aussi

I WONDER WHERE MY BABY IS TONIGHT

I burned up every letter
And thought that I'd feel better

I put away her picture, too
Sent back each little present
And though it wasn't pleasant
It seemed the wisest thing to do
I've done everything I could do and yet
It isn't easy to forget
I wonder where my baby is tonight
I wonder how my baby is tonight

JE ME DEMANDE OÙ EST MA PETITE CE SOIR?

J'ai brûlé toutes les lettres
Et pense que mon cœur serait plus tranquille
J'ai enlevé tous ses portraits aussi
Je me suis débarrassé des petits cadeaux
Et quoique ce fut très douloureux
Il m'a semblé que la plus grande chose à faire
Je l'avais faite et même plus encore
Mais ce n'est pas si facile que cela d'oublier
Je me demande où est ma petite ce soir
Je me demande comment est ma petite ce soir

ALWAYS

Everything went wrong
And the whole day long

I'd feel so blue
For the longest while
I'd forget to smile

ALWAYS

Chaque chose allait mal et tout le long du jour
J'étais si mélancolique
Depuis un temps très long
J'avais oublié mon sourire

A song isn't a string of melodies you unwind with a stiff smile and your nose in the air, nor is it a lament—not an exercise for the foolhardy, either. It's a comedy, a tragedy, a set of movements, a play of poses. Or, ignoring convention: a silly expression and your hand on your heart.

Like sculpting in the air with the music. You've got to let the music mold you. Your body has to follow your voice, help it express the music. You also sing with your knees, your elbows, your shoulders, everything. To do it well, every song should have its own costume, hairstyle, and makeup; the right kind of light; matching scenery.

You have to squeeze a song from all sides, like a lemon.

With a chorus, you can furnish even the biggest of stages. That doesn't mean you should leap around like a frog. For example, at the Casino de Paris, I wanted to sing on my knees, alone, at center stage. I triumphed. But the pose has to be true, Monsieur Sauvage.

When everything is fake, nothing works. The audience wants to hear your heart beating in the silence between two notes. They're touched by the sound of your heartbeat. You go up the scale, you keep climbing it, all the way to the top—and then, nothing. Or you go all the way down, and then nothing. Nothing but people breathing as they listen. That second of silence when everyone's heart beats as one might be the most difficult thing to achieve in a song. An artist only gets there through hard work—when work doesn't kill precisely what is special about them: spontaneity.

My inspiration in this regard, as for many others, is an extraordinary woman, a living legend: Mistinguett. It's interesting that the cabaret artists who have mocked her so often fail to point out that she's never aged. She's always at her best in one way or another. Her work and her commitment to work have been astounding, as is her perseverance with life and with her art that's been honed with so much care, learned directly from real life.

When I'm so tired or fed up that I'm on the verge of giving up and throwing it all away sometimes, I think about Mistinguett. I pull myself together. I accept things. I tell myself I have to carry on, work hard like her, follow her example, her lust for life. Unfortunately, in our generation, I don't think we'll see anyone who could replace her.

When Miss, the great Mistinguett, attends a show as an audience member, you can judge, by the cheers she immediately gets when they announce she's there, the place she still holds in the audience's hearts.

And since people make up so many stories about her, I want to tell you something true. She was wonderfully good to her family. All the rest is just misunderstandings or rumors.

✦   ✦   ✦

I apologize, Monsieur Sauvage, for laying so much store by the quality of the man or the woman within an artist, especially their innate kindness.

What interests me most is the cry from within. Édith Piaf had a cry that came from her flesh: the cry of the Little Sparrow. I may not be the right person to talk about what made her art so original. I'm not French enough by training to fully appreciate the impact of her accent. I wasn't born in the faubourgs of Paris. But she's definitely the most *womanly* of our chanteuses, Édith Piaf.

We lunched together at her American cabaret. It was my first time meeting her in private. Still humble, sensitive, frank, she won me over. I admire her. She's a good person as far as I can tell, from the one long conversation we had.

Why can't people see that there's not enough kindness these days? Our world isn't so much in poor taste as entirely unacceptable. We can't carry on like this. I personally feel like I'm walking on shifting sands when I think about everything that needs to be put right, to be transformed with kindness.

Consider low-grade staff: who looks after them with any affection? It isn't machines that'll fix the situation, you know.

Young artists—for example, newcomers—go through nothing but hardship. It's all well and good to say that young girls, seventeen-year-olds, have a burning passion, especially for the theater, but that flame doesn't put food on the table. They're paid so badly. They're made to resort to desperate measures. Life is expensive, so they have to become anyone's little mistress just to carry on.

The big directors are very guilty of this. They're condemning their own futures and all the arts, they're condemning them all. My soul is sick of it. It's a haunting shame. It's as if I were responsible. It drains my joy in being alive and successful.

A song, you see—whether it's sad or funny, mournful, *olé olé*, whatever—is a lullaby that we cling on to throughout life . . . It's a hope, an open window—even the most open people are never open enough.

Puisque tout doit finir un jour ou l'autre
Tâchons au moins de ne pas trop faiblir . . .

Since everything must end one day or another
Let's at least try not to waste away so . . .

A song . . . A play you stage. A theatrical character you voice. But first you need a stroke of luck, a melody with its context, the chorus that finds its way. I was lucky that Vincent Scotto found melodies for me that fitted what I wanted to say when I was starting out. First, the music—lyrics, on the other hand, are generally so poor. Why don't poets write more songs? Why do most singers not act what they're singing anymore? It doesn't sound right. It's lifeless.

Theater is the dancing reflection of life, of its excitement, perhaps, but above all it is a transposition that's always faithful. Sacha Guitry made me understand that better than anyone. Guitry is the truest great theater star I know. I have infinite admiration for him in this business. I see actors who live artificial lives, pretentious, as if they were still onstage, acting stupidly. They're bad actors either way. But he's like a fish in water in the theater. Onstage, he's alive. And in real life, it's like he's watching true theater . . . How can I express it? He keeps the human touch, with style.

I understood him. He understood me, too, even though I looked so different. He knew I was an actress, not a colored frog. He said so to Monsieur Willemetz and Madame Volterra. And thanks to his advice, I performed—well—in Offenbach's musical *La Créole*, for ten months.

The preview night took place on December 15, 1934.

Do you know the gangster Jo-la-Terreur? That was me. I had to explode with a towering rage. I smashed dishes, bowls, and vases every night for ten months. The pieces would scatter all over the stage . . . Imagine the cost these days! But the ceramics and porcelain at the Marigny were made of plaster.

Those were good times. The costume I wore had enormous sleeves that reminded me of the dresses with trains and gigot sleeves I'd borrow from my grandmother's supply, when I'd dress up in St. Louis, in the cellar of our house. And I could laugh here, and sing, babble, pull faces, thumb my nose, dance, make bird sounds, or roar as much as I liked!

Souviens-toi de la Jamaïque . . .
Remember Jamaica . . .

It all ended with a lullaby when I left my heart and my breath to die.

I had abandoned Paris for a year and a half for a series of tours around the country. I was so happy to see my great Paris audience again, and even happier to be back in a *theater*-theater, with an audience that was like family, who didn't think I was just a musical curiosity who emerged onstage with feathers, a dance, and a song. I was performing. I had a role. I was leading the entire plot of a play.

Messieurs Albert Willemetz and Georges Delance had indulgently revised Albert Milhaud's libretto and sprinkled Offenbach's music with songs taken from his other works. It was reshaped just for me; they'd added a ballet; they re-energized and humanized the old operetta.

My performance turned out to be an American tribute to Offenbach. We merged the two together. I tried to make my character as natural as possible, and to show all the talents I was already recognized for.

In the third act, my gawky figure was probably reminiscent of my youthful beginnings. At least, I imagined, my friends could see how far I'd come, appreciate what the American girl from *La Revue Nègre* had achieved in ten years. I now spoke French. I performed in French, alongside essentially French actors: Dréan, Urban, Adrien Lamy, René Charles, Rose Carday. Madame Volterra's stage direction was very French in taste, the best kind, I think.

French comedy is of a much higher quality than American burlesque. But who doesn't have their vanity? I admit that I do. In all the shows I starred in, and the films, too, I wanted to evoke different stages of my life. I want to try something new every time, but—forgive me for how proud this makes me feel—every time there should also be a reminder of the past, some sort of indication, for contrast.

La Créole is a journey, set in the past, from Jamaica to La Rochelle. And ultimately, everything I've done goes back to my own adventure from downtown St. Louis, America, to downtown Paris. I couldn't forget it. I'm proud of it. Am I wrong, or am I right?

But the most entertaining thing about *La Créole* were the swarms of children; they brought fresh air to the play. I'd give them a snack on Sundays. What a joy, if only you'd seen it! And since the little girls told their mothers, *they* also started coming, more and more, every Sunday. They would bring their newborns to me. My dressing room was full of newborn babies singing, oh, là là! I was like a nursemaid with all these little pink, screaming bundles. There were bottles everywhere. It was wonderful, *La Créole*.

Yes, songs have a soul. You've got to give them a soul and feed that soul. That's where their value lies. But sometimes a song's soul chokes you.

When I was in Germany, at the end of the war, when the prison camps were being liberated, the people at the top were looking for someone who'd be willing to sing in one of the most dreadful death camps, a camp full of typhoid.

While the poor souls there—the dying, skeletons, ghosts with burning fevers—waited to be transported out of the camp, someone needed to try and distract them, restore their hope, to console them, or at least save them first from despair. I volunteered. It was in the nature of my mission. Imagine: the moment they knew their liberators were there, close by, dozens and dozens of these prisoners brought from all over the world dragged themselves to the edges of the camp, to the barbed wire, and clung on to it; they died right there from the effort, on their knees, their hands in shreds, their eyes wide open.

The others went on waiting.

They couldn't move; most of them were dying. I've never seen anything more dreadful. I knew most of them were going to die.

The camp was in a small valley surrounded by trees, hidden in the middle of greenery. Nobody knew—there was no way to have known—that it was there. Those living nearby swore they'd never known about it. But there they were, these poor souls deported to their slow deaths, lying on wooden boards when I arrived. They were smiling despite everything. They were trying . . . They were wearing armbands with the Cross of Lorraine on their skinny arms. I felt so choked with tears but I didn't want to cry. I read the dates, the names, and the notes on the planks: the names of the poor dead lying next to the living . . . I had to smile. I had to sing. I sang "Dans Mon Village" to each group in those shacks, quietly, as if I were singing to each individual. And the song choked me:

Dans mon village . . .
Chaque clocher des environs
Chaque sentier, chaque buisson . . .

In my village . . .
Every clock tower nearby
Every field, every bush . . .

I saw them, the clock towers, in the eyes of these dying people. I heard the sound of the bells in their wheezing breaths. It helped me find my voice again. I put my whole heart into the song, with so much love, so much sincerity, so much persuasion this time that, at the end, we all cried—but not because we were sad; no, we were no longer sad.

I had already sung this song so often in camps in Africa and Italy, in French and in English, that the lyrics weren't important anymore. I'd change and adapt them as I liked.

Now it was just the soul of a song, you understand?

I can sing in French, English, Portuguese, Spanish, Italian, and German. I've learned these languages to different degrees, enough to understand them and not get the accent wrong, their nuances. When one has sung a song in many languages, only then is it right for everyone. Whatever was too particular about it, too specific, banal, in the words, it all disappears.

But I had a different experience with Schubert's "Ave Maria."

It amazes so many people that Josephine Baker sings this song, that she likes singing it. And I like it, you know! The words are in Latin. I've been told what they mean but I still don't understand them. And so few people do. I think they're all the more moved by the spirit of the music. I hope so, and that it helps them to better feel what I want to express about myself, in my way, beyond the song . . .

Monsieur Sauvage, I'm going to tell you where I found the softness, the sincerity, the grace of the "Ave Maria" that I hope I will always keep.

In Egypt, in Cairo, I knew an orthodox Jesuit, Reverend Father Ayrout. He set up some charity work over there for the villagers—the *fellahs*—of the Upper Nile. They were living—dying—in incredible misery. I really was amazed that a Jesuit father, and one known to be a scholar at that, was interested in a singer who was just passing through. A young lawyer introduced us, a friend of Mr. Hassan Mazhar Bey, director of press at the Foreign Ministry, who's since become an ambassador in Europe. Since the Reverend was kind to me, and so understanding, I asked if I could attend one of his Masses and, if he would allow me, to sing the "Ave Maria" there. He said yes right away.

A few days later, very early in the morning, I found myself in the little chapel he'd set up by himself in a corner of his apartment. There were two lit candles on the simple altar, a few flowers, in that austere house with almost no furniture.

There were seven at Mass. I sang the "Ave Maria" while the Reverend Father conducted the ceremony. I was thinking about the poor Egyptian villagers, about the priest who devoted himself to the White Madonna and the Black Madonna for their sake.

It was in this little chapel that I found the tone for my "Ave Maria." Now I can sing it anywhere. I'm back in Cairo, in front of that humble altar.

I've already told you that my adventure from the banks of the Mississippi to the banks of the Seine is always there in my mind.

But whatever hardship I've had through the years, don't you think it's been a great adventure, a happy one despite everything, in so many ways?

I still sing the "Ave Maria," in another way, at the Club des Champs-Élysées as part of *Mon Beau Livre d'Images*. It's a book of illustrations by Albert Dubout—eight drawings that we present to the audience one by one. Every time I look at one of the drawings, I have a crazy urge to laugh and make jokes. And I do. I don't know where Dubout got his Negroes from, but they're funnier than me. They make me laugh and scare me a little. But not as much as making a record or going on the radio.

I made a new series of records with Pacific, with accompaniment by Jo Bouillon and his orchestra.[12] The people were nice, of course, but the devices that run from mouth to mouth were a real bother, devices that drink the music right from your lips; it's like they want to suck you up whole: electric wires, cables, microphones that go up and down like big spiders, the technicians watching you . . . Oh, là là! I can't get used to it. How can I feel good about all that machinery? And another thing: I don't like canned food, and by that I mean I don't like being put in a can. I do love records, though. But these days, when I hear a record playing Josephine Baker, I ask them to stop it right away. On the radio it's worse. I turn it off as soon as I hear my voice. I get so nervous with a microphone. My voice shakes. For a little while, I sounded like a goat in labor.

Monsieur Gilson thinks it all went fine. He's a poet, Monsieur Gilson. I came across him in Mexico, this lovely poet of the radio.

"You'll perform every week on French radio," he said.

I didn't want to upset him or Monsieur Porché, especially

because French radio—we might like to complain about it, but when you know what foreign radio is like, believe me—it's still the best. It's one hundred times livelier and freer. I'm not talking about the machines but the men. Our radio is cheerful; in other places it's all too much, wheels within wheels, business, advertising pieces. It's frightening. It puts me off.

When I don't have an audience in front of me, I really feel lost.

Television is different. You can move, dance, become yourself again. I know they can see me when they're listening to me. In England, I featured in the first big television show—*Café Continental*—and in Paris in October '48, I was part of a televised gala in honor of the UN world congress. But, for me, nothing ever beats the glow of backstage, of treading the boards, the theater, my audience, my friends who've come out.

FOUR YEARS OF ADVENTURE

In the Service of France on the Sidelines
of the Second World War

There were four long years between the Château des Milandes, which I'd rented before the war, and Si Mohamed Menebhi's palace in Marrakesh, where I lived, where I took shelter between my different run-ins with adventure.

It was the Second World War.

It was miserable; iron in the soul.

It wasn't the time to be stuck in bed, to be unwell. "Don't move. Rest. One more month . . . One more week."

It's so silly, what happened to me.

When your belly gets opened up thirty-six times why don't they just give you a zipper? Then you could open it, take a look, and close it again. Just like that! Then they wouldn't have to cut you open all the time to see what's wrong.

During those years, I had far too many encounters with bistoury knives, clinics, sleepless nights, fevers. I heard every one of the muezzin's calls to prayer. I believe that Muslims are the people closest to God. They prayed for me. I survived.

The Château des Milandes—which belongs to me now—is near Sarlat, in Dordogne, in Castelnaud-Fayrac. It's an old, fifteenth-century château with one part that's a little older, from the twelfth century. It's often been restored, ever since it's existed up there on the hill between the trees, but it's kept its historic air and its watchtowers. It looks over the trees and this corner of the valley where the Dordogne flows peacefully. I could tell you everything that's happened to it since it was born. I've read a lot about it, about its first era and the other ones, too. While I was unwell in Africa, I asked for lots of books on the Middle Ages, the Crusades, the old French châteaux and chevaliers, and the lords of Castelnaud, les Milandes, Montfort, and Beynac.

One night, in the month of October 1940, a chevalier with a small suitcase came to see me at the Château des Milandes. It was Jack Sanders.

"'Jack Sanders'?"

"Yes, 'Captain Fox' is dead. And soon 'Jack Sanders' will be, too. He'll use that to get ten years older before being reborn. He'll be called Jacques-François Hébert . . . Don't forget."

My friend Jack was a clandestine crusader. Captain Jacques Abtey, of the Second Bureau of the General Staff. He was the companion that Providence sent me. He was the best in a team not lacking in crusaders, serving France and France alone.

What would I have done without them? Maybe I helped them. But they helped me even more. We did what we could, did our best. But what a pounding heart, oh, là là! Can you imagine me, Monsieur Sauvage, slipping around like an eel, with little secret papers, like curlers, gently pinned under my dress?

But wait, this is just the beginning.

When I first met Captain Abtey, he went by the name of "Captain Fox"—at the start of the war. I also know his whole family: his wife, his children. I really love them.

He came tiptoeing to Beau Chêne, my house in Le Vésinet that would later be occupied by the Germans—they sabotaged it. The Americans and French who lived there after didn't fix the damage much.

I only asked for one thing, the smallest thing: to serve the country to which I would always owe a debt of gratitude, even if I had to give my life. France made me who I am, despite all the prejudices.

But I wasn't a spy. It's not in my nature, you know that. I was in the IPSA, the nurse pilots of the health services, working for the Red Cross. Madame Schneider assigned me to look after Belgian refugees. At first I was in a white coat on Rue du Chevaleret, in an old homeless shelter, where they were sending floods and floods of miserable refugees. Some of them, however, looked suspicious, some black sheep mixed in with the flocks of poor souls.

I had my eye on them.

And my ear, too.

Because an Italian embassy attaché had also got into the habit of whispering in my ear. You could say he told me some very interesting things. I passed them on to Captain Fox, or "Petz," as his comrades called him. He was pleased.

Then I took cover at the Château des Milandes, where we

stayed warm even though autumn had started to put a chill in the air. This was September '40 . . . Bang, bang, bang . . . Someone was knocking as if they wanted to break the door down. It was a German soldier, along with a petty officer, stiff as a mannequin, a non-commissioned officer behind him, and three green uniforms, with rifles.

"You are concealing arms in this château . . . We know."

Oh, là là! This man was so proper, so cool, ready for anything. His minions were guarding the doors. But there were no arms in the château.

Phew!

An armchair is just what you need after a visit like that!

Jack told me that the SR—the famous Service de Renseignements, the French intelligence service—was in the middle of a major reorganization and that the CE—Contre-espionnage, the counterintelligence service—should still be working, but in a different way. He said the IS, the British Intelligence Service, wasn't half bad and that in these conditions, the star Josephine Baker could take care of some undercover agents.

Okay, kids. I'll put together a wonderful tour. You'll be flute players. Jack is an artist, definitely. He was a ballet master.

Let's go: next stops Spain, Portugal, Brazil. After that, we'll see. We saw firsthand that they didn't give out passports like Metro tickets, even to decent folk. And the trains hardly moved until they reached the border. They never went fast enough.

Toulouse, Lourdes, Tarbes, Pau, the Pyrenees, the line of customs officers.

"Passports, please . . ."

Everything was going well.

There was a lovely Douglas plane at Barajas airport in Madrid—surrounded by a dozen sinister birds holding swastikas. Mechanics in blue overalls were busy with our airplane. They were nice to me and my group.

The rotors were spinning . . .

Time to go!

I buried my nose in my fur coat; it was funny. But what was that? A little Spanish airplane was zipping around us, doing acrobatics, brushing right past us really fast, flying up, coming back. It was going to crash into us at any moment. What did it want, this tiny thing? Nothing . . . Eventually, it left, the pest.

The moon was below us, among the clouds.

When we opened the cabin door, we were in Portugal. In Sintra. It was sunny. People were smiling. There was no war here. The young people on the street were wrapped in black cloaks that were all ragged. We learned they were from Coimbra, the old university where rips and shreds were in style—it was symbolic poverty. You've got to poke fun at wealth if you want to keep your knowledge pure.

There I was in Lisbon, at Hotel Aviz. Time to catch my breath. The hotel was full of journalists . . . "But I have nothing to say, I assure you. I've come to dance and sing. I'm going to Rio because I have to, for an ongoing commitment, that's all."

Those darn journalists! The next day, my photo was on the front page of all the newspapers. Without meaning to, I'd dethroned

King Carol of Romania and the Negus's son, who were also in Portugal.

Then it was over, the trip to Brazil. News was waiting for us in Lisbon—a telegram from London. They wanted to put together a new liaison unit in France.

So it was goodbye, Lisbon, even though Jack kept telling me I was going to come back and he was going to prepare our quarters on the other side of the sea. The Spanish ambassador, the caudillo's brother, came in handy for this, for the papers.

The December sky scared me, a little. But I still got back in the airplane. We didn't have a minute to lose.

Monsieur Paillole was there in Marseille—a link in the chain, so to speak. I passed on the news. Then I went back. I had no more money and I didn't want to use anyone's but my own. One shouldn't expect pay when working for France, you see? I had also sworn to myself that I wouldn't sing in France as long as there was a single German there. But how would I manage it? I didn't know.

Monsieur Paillole spoke up.

"Return to your artistic work. It's essential. There's no better cover for you," he said.

My cover was *La Créole*, which I had performed in Paris, before the war, from 1934 to 1935 at Théâtre Marigny.

I sorted things out with the people at the Opéra de Marseille. I accepted their proposition. In ten days, I'd prepared Offenbach's musical for the stage and rehearsed a role I hadn't thought about for six years. And quickly, quickly, I got everyone to rehearse their roles with me. At the same time, we were advertising around the city: "Josephine Baker, in Offenbach's *La Créole*, 24th December 1940, with the municipal theater company."

And I sang: *Souviens-toi de la Jamaïque . . . Remember Jamaica . . .*

Meanwhile, Jack appeared out of the blue. He'd met Mr. Bacon in Lisbon, an Englishman—an oddball. He was counting on us to establish a link between France and Morocco, with a little sailboat that would travel back and forth between Lisbon and Casablanca.

Finis to *La Créole*.

No more music allowed in Marseille.

However, according to my contract, I still had to give a performance in Montpellier and another in Béziers. Impossible. They needed us in Africa. I wasn't a volunteer agent anymore. I was a full-fledged servicewoman, retrospectively, as from the month of November. Without a rank and without pay—I didn't want them. Second class. And . . . forward march! One has to earn one's stripes.

In Marseille, at the Hôtel de Noailles on La Canebière, I was packing my bags and coughing. I had a terrible cold. And it would get worse still. I needed a doctor's certificate to legally put the rest of my performances on hold. So I went. I had an X-ray. Then the doctor examined me with a stethoscope, once, twice, and looked at me with wide eyes.

"I say, Mademoiselle, this is serious. I can't lie to you. There are shadows in the top area of both your lungs, the start of a serious congestion. Leave this cold country at once. You're in dire need of some sun."

It was bitterly cold in Marseille. The whole of France, actually, was frozen under the snow. Nineteen forty-one was off to a difficult start. My dear animals were waiting for me at the Château des Milandes. I couldn't abandon them. No, sir. I'll do whatever you want, but I won't abandon an animal who trusts me.

Wouldn't someone go and get my little animals?

The lovely Bayonne, who was acting as the manager in our team, brought them from the château. Oh, là là! What joy.

There was Glouglou, my lady monkey, a clever thing, who loved looking for fleas. She'd even look for them in my fur coats and the bristles of my brush. There was Mica, a golden lion tamarin, very serious, no bigger than a baby cat. There was Gugusse, the marmoset, with his little mustache. He was a real piece of work, but a sweetheart. There were two little girls: Mademoiselle Bigoudi and Mademoiselle Point d'Interrogation, my little white mice, who were delighted. Mice have feelings, you know. And they're flirts, you wouldn't believe it. Finally, of the larger kind, there was my dog Bonzo, a Great Dane, enormous. He was sweet, as long as you didn't look at him the wrong way.

This little group was so happy at the Hôtel de Noailles! And I was, too! Bonzo lying on the hotel room rug with a mouse cleaning itself on the end of his nose; Gugusse on a visit to the wardrobe; Glouglou in the curtains, climbing with his little hands; Mica in the middle of the bed, like a real miniature lion in a dish of cream.

Poor dears! It was a big adventure for them, too. Let's go . . . Everyone together.

Now it was time to put them back in their baskets.

I'll always remember the crossing from Marseille to Algiers on the *Gouverneur Général de Gueydon*. And what weather, Monsieur

Sauvage! My poor animals! They didn't know what a storm was. They sure learned. My Glouglou's eyes went dull. Gugusse was nibbling at his little mustache to comfort himself.

But when we arrived, the sky was blue, the city of a thousand balconies all pink, from floor to floor, in the pale morning sun.

"Are you Madame Josephine Baker?"

"Yes, Monsieur!"

"Follow me, please. I have a complaint against you."

The inspector was doing his job. But I made a face . . . Arrest me? Why?

Well! Because, quite simply, having put their business heads back on and now attending to nothing besides their own patriotic bravado, the management at the Opéra de Marseille theater—to whom we had explained ourselves very clearly, mind you—had denounced me for breach of contract and abandoning the company and was asking me for four hundred thousand francs in compensation.

How nice of them! But this low blow backfired: for the entire week that I stayed in Algiers, I took part in a gala for the air force.

I was waiting to leave for Casablanca.

I would write letters to consuls on behalf of my scattered companions who were waiting in the shadows for me to facilitate their missions. And at night as I hunched over my papers in the Aletti Hotel, I confess I never imagined that I would soon be going to Marrakesh, then Agadir, then from Agadir to Fez, and then from Fez—a city that sings under your feet because of the underground streams—back to Spain, then Portugal, then back to Morocco, then again to Tlemcen and Algiers, then later from Algiers to Tunis, Tripoli, Benghazi; from Benghazi to Alexandria, to Cairo;

from Cairo to Jerusalem, Jaffa, Haifa, Damascus; and from Damascus to Beirut, or that I'd have to travel thousands and thousands of kilometers across desert sands; along roads full of mines; past dead airplanes, burned cars, battlefields, and cemeteries in a little jeep with the crusaders for Free France. Oh, I was so far from imagining all that! And far, too, from predicting that for months and months I would be between life and death, but in a different way—with my belly cut open. So far from predicting I'd be in Africa for years.

But there had been signs. Gugusse hadn't come back from a trip into the hotel's gutters. My white mice, my two little Mademoiselles, had disappeared. I was downcast.

Does one ever know what one will do?

And so, no sooner had I arrived in Casablanca than I had to take the train to Tangier, with a suitcase stuffed with ordinary-looking papers and theater programs, but there was something else between the lines, written with water, you know, invisible water. I took that suitcase to Lisbon; that was my first mission. I was glowing and very well-behaved. Ah, yes! Good as gold. His Excellency Menebhi's brother, Abderrahman, and His Highness Moulay Larbi el Alaoui's friends, including His Excellency Bel Bachir, were there to protect me and guide me, so kindly; they had such authority over everyone. People cheered when they saw Bel Bachir on the street. They'd shout his name.

The officials in Tétouan organized a big dinner in my honor. If only they'd known! As for me, I was listening. I didn't miss a thing. The Spanish officials were gossiping to each other. Josephine was light-years away from all that—or so they thought! To top all this, they lavished me with presents; the most valuable was a permanent transit visa for Spain.

Unfortunately, I had hardly any luck in Lisbon, despite a few successful performances—still a cover. What I mean is that Jack didn't manage to get my fixer to do what he had so wanted.

Marrakesh, Monsieur Sauvage, the Pearl of the South, where white Africa and black Africa meet . . . The legendary palm trees, the old city walls and their studded doors, the Agdal, the fountains with their clear water, the great leaders' tombs, the mosques. It's as if all the nomads deep in the desert had been dreaming of something like this for centuries.

I had such a beautiful time there, a painful time, too. No matter where I went in Africa, I'd always go back there . . . For four years. I'd take shelter there when I was weary, too weary to go on.

The wind rushes down from the Atlas Mountains around the Koutoubia, the Muslims' cathedral, in the Red City, *Medinet el-Hamra,* as the old Moroccans say.

"Balek, balek." Donkey drivers trot barefoot next to their animals, asking you to make way.

"Allah yjib . . ." May Allah provide for you, they say to the poor people.

And there are so many poor people! You don't know what poverty is until you know poor Muslims.

The Jemaa el-Fna is a square just teeming with people! Extreme poverty in rags, and the flea market. Meat stalls black with flies . . . bread sellers squatting side by side. It's a meeting place for curious people, photographers, snake charmers, and storytellers. Teeming in the dust. Singing in the sun. Haggling. Shouting. Yelling. Smells of fried food, cinnamon, and mint, spices, wizards' and healers' concoctions, herbs, drugs, drying birds' heads, rotting monkeys' feet.

And the open-air barbers tilt their clients' heads back over brass dishes. A sweep of the lancet on either side of the nape. They chatter while the bad blood drains out. It's bloodletting time at Jemaa el-Fna. Do you know what it means: Jemaa el-Fna? Square of the Dead. It's where they used to put rebels' heads on display, in the past.

Every day in this big open space, it was a battle of clandestine propaganda. Documents were passed from hand to hand under the burnooses.

Then we'd go to the souk.

I'd go shopping in the souk, among the crowd. The merchants knew me, in their little stalls like shops for bees. The little children with their big eyes would shout "S'phine, S'phine . . ." I was dressed like a Muslim but without a piece of fabric over my mouth. First the Arabs quietly grumbled, then they started calling me Little Sister. But sometimes I'd come to blows with them because they're too harsh with their animals. They were raised so harshly themselves, I know.

First, I lived in La Mamounia Hotel, it's famous, in the Bab El-Djedid area. Then I wanted to have my own house, to live like the Arabs. I found one in the Medina, near the Koutoubia, with its three golden balls raised high above the city's flat roofs. It was at the end of a narrow blind alley, lost, squeezed in between the walls.

You had to knock three times on the little, low door, with the knocker. And my servant would open it for you. He'd wear a gandoura, all white like his long beard. He'd greet you by putting his big, skinny, yellow hand over his heart. The dark hallway was covered in blue mosaic tiles to maintain a cool glow; at the end, you'd see another small, low door. Behind it was the garden of Allah. There were orange trees that always had oranges, around a fountain where the birds would come to drink. And there were marble pillars, as slim as young girls, and deep shadows. From here you could enter any way you liked. All the doors stood open onto the patio, which was like a block of light shining up to the sky. All you had to do was lift one of the curtains hanging in the arches.

And five times a day, from dawn to the middle of the night, I'd hear the muezzin's melodic and rather husky voice, singing for prayer from the top of the nearby mosque: "La illaha illa Allah . . ."

Next, I accepted Si Mohamed Menebhi's hospitality—later, during our main excursion across the Muslim world, from Marrakesh to Damascus, he would become another magnificent and generous chevalier for the French cause. May God reward him for everything he did for France and everything he did for me in his forefathers' palace at the end of that little road, Derb Allilich. His three daughters have a place in my heart: Fela, Rafet, Hagdousch . . . We wore woolen jellabas together, so soft.

I'll sing you a song of remembrance that is dear to me now, dearer than any other song of remembrance, because it includes his wife's name: Zoubida . . . [13]

Le matin où s'en vont les rêves

Où s'en vont les étoiles du soir

Aussitôt que le jour se lève

Où donc va l'amour? Oh! coursier noir!

La nuit se lève et je chante

Pour mieux retrouver ta jolie peau

Ta belle main caressante

Et ton regard sombre et si beau.

Oh! Sidi

Allah . . .

Oh! Sidi

Allah . . .

In the morning, when dreams go on their way

When the evening stars go

Just as day is breaking

Then does love go? Oh, dark messenger!

Night is rising and I sing

To recall the touch of your pretty skin

The touch of your lovely hand

And your dark, enchanting eyes.

Oh! Sidi

Allah . . .

Oh! Sidi

Allah . . .

And I'll never forget, either, how devoted his servants were, by the names of Aïcha, Lamber, and Ourika, with their flowery babouche slippers.

Let me linger in Marrakesh a little, before the time I became unwell. From autumn until spring, you see the mountains covered with snow and the little streams flowing between the tall palm trees, like masts on a ship with a bouquet of palm leaves on top.

One night during my first stay, our friend Moulay Larbi told us that according to intelligence from Tétouan, there were fears that Morocco would be attacked by an expeditionary force of Spaniards and Germans.

How would we find out what was going on?

The next day I was in Casablanca; the day after that, in Tangier. From there, I left for a three-week tour in Spain. I performed in Barcelona, pressed on to Madrid. And, naturally, I didn't turn down any invitation from the embassies, the consuls, the worthies who would talk. When I came back, I was stuffed with messages, wearing little secret papers, paper tickets, almost everywhere.

I couldn't wait to return to Marrakesh. But I made a stop in Casablanca so a doctor could examine me. My bronchitis was no joke, you know, in Marseille. I had been feeling its effects for a long time. Apparently I was cured, but there were no guarantees. Plus, I wanted to know for certain if I could have children. That was my obsession. Isn't a woman's goal in life, whoever she is, to have children? That's why I got X-rayed by a specialist. A serious one—you'll see.

In my little house in Marrakesh, a few days later, I had a raging fever and ice, a pack of crushed ice held in rubber, on my belly.

The diagnosis: "Risk of peritonitis, infection following the radiologist's injection."

Jack was scared. In the night, on doctor's orders, my colleagues drove me back to Casablanca. It was upsetting to see them, my brave colleagues! I could tell from their fake smiles that they were even more worried than me.

Voilà. They put me to sleep. Doctor Comte operated on me; he saved me. But I stayed in a clinic for nineteen months after that, from June 1941 to December 1942. Life in a hospital bed with the smell of ether; it's slow. And I was thinking about my animals. I would have liked them to be there so I could tell them things you can only say to animals. I thought about Gigolo, who'd died in his cage the winter before. I found him dead, my little African sparrow, all stiff with his little feet lifted to the sky.

Instead, I watched the shadows moving over the ceiling of the clinic. I waited.

But bad luck can still come in handy. My sick room in Casablanca turned into an intelligence center, a peaceful meeting place for men who needed to talk quietly about the future.

✦ ✦ ✦

If only you'd seen my legs! They'd wasted away in three weeks. I didn't want anyone to see them. They were really, really skinny. I wore a long yellow dress to hide them when they let me stand up for the first time. And suddenly, I didn't know how to walk anymore. I couldn't do it. She used to be so beautiful, did Josephine Baker, oh, là là! A dancer who can't stand up on her sticks anymore. I had to relearn how to stand straight, like this, one foot in front of the other, surrounded by nurses. But I still went round to see the other patients: "Look, everybody, you'll get better, too . . . It's all right . . . Don't worry."

I thought I was stronger than I was. I accepted an invitation to visit some friends in Rabat. It would do me good to spend some of my convalescence in the shadow of Hassan Tower, which looked like the big mosque in Marrakesh. The Oudaya Gardens are paradise.

Dear me . . . I was far from convalescing! Three days later—I was so happy the United States had finally declared war on the Germans—I had a fever of forty. Here we go again. More peritonitis, more diets, more needles, more sulfonamides. I improved my vocabulary at the clinic: lapse and relapse. What's tachycardia again? The devil and all his friends come to play havoc in my body. Doctor Bolot wasn't happy. Neither was I.

Then it was Christmas 1941. In a corner of my room, on a table, little multicolored candles were burning at the tips of the branches of a little tree.

Christmas, for me, is the best holiday, the happiest time for little children. I think of all the little ones in the world and of my own childhood. The day before Christmas, I would clean the snow off the steps of the houses in St. Louis to earn a few cents: two for the long flights of steps, one for the rest. I'd use that to buy little things for the Christmas tree and for my little friends who were poor like me. I've always celebrated Christmas for the children. The poorest of them should be able to enjoy it the most, have all the toys. Their happiness at Christmas is always mine, too; I give as much as I can, what could be better?

Meanwhile, I wasn't fine at all. Doctor Comte, who'd just got back from a trip, taught me a new word: "septicemia." "A one in five chance . . ." And another very ominous word: "obstruction." To my great joy, I had an intestinal obstruction. I was blocked right up. But then Jack came, Jack, my guardian angel during these terrible times. And we prayed.

One morning, in spring '42, there was a knocking on the window. Thousands of little taps. Well, come in! Someone open the window. It was locusts. The sky was filled with them. An invasion of big locusts, yellow and black and shiny, with dancer's legs and long, transparent wings. I tried to tame one. But apparently it can't be done. The nurse squashed my locust.

Well you're an old locust yourself, Miss Nurse!

And as the weeks passed, I would read history books when the injections weren't hurting me too much.

Another morning, in the month of June, June 28, 1942, at nine in the morning, I was taken once more to the operating theater. What a way to wake up! Such a thick tongue, a really heavy tongue . . . And I was thirsty! I drank for eight days. Then I was hungry.

But it was going too well, too nicely . . . A touch of embolism came to bother me . . . Oh! Darn it, darn it, darn it . . .

Fortunately, Mademoiselle Marie Rochas was watching over me, otherwise the embolism would have completely finished me off.

Also, luckily Saki arrived to distract me. I'd already heard him meowing. But it was such a small, tiny cry, so far away, even more so since it was operation day for me again. I wasn't quite in my right mind. I heard someone whining, that's all.

Poor little thing! His legs could hardly carry him. He fell over and curled into a ball. He rolled around; his head was bigger than his little, mangy belly. He had hardly any fur. Where in the clinic had he come from? Animals weren't allowed. He must have guessed I was here. I immediately claimed him. Bring me that cat. The nurse made him a little space in my room. People called him "Fleabag." But I named him Saki. He liked that better. And I started knitting him a jumper.

"Hello, Saki?"

He opened his eyes, stuck out his little tongue. He was no bigger than a rat.

"Hello, Saki?"

This kitten had long, pointy ears to hear me with. I saved him. I'm a good animal doctor. All they need is a little affection, like people. The whole of life is a matter of affection that one has or doesn't have.

But he scared me the first time he jumped on my bed. I was sleeping. He woke me with a start.

What's wrong this morning, Saki? There was bombing from all sides at once. It was November 8, 1942. The Americans were landing. Just enough time to grab my dressing gown, and then we were on the terrace outside the clinic. We stayed there for around three days and three nights.

On November 11, the American soldiers and the French soldiers marched side by side through the streets of Casablanca. I was standing to attention. I wept. I couldn't hug them all.

I was a soldier, but Soldier Baker's secret mission had now come to an end. So I thought. Besides, I was still too weak to guarantee my service amid the battles. It made me furious.

On December 1, I went back to Marrakesh, to La Mamounia Hotel. At least this year, I thought, I can celebrate Christmas properly with some friends and lots of children around me.

One shouldn't make vows, you know. But that's what I wanted. It would have done me good. Do you know where I was at Christmas? In bed, with a kind of typhoid fever.

In the end, what can you do?

Give up?

Let yourself die?

Oh! No.

As soon as my fever had reduced a little, I went to Si Mene-bhi's. I mulled over all this in his palace—in a pretty guesthouse just for me. I wasn't feeling very happy. When you're not happy, you should be anyway. You should sing—there's no better remedy—even if you're shaking like a leaf, even if your belly is cut open.

Mine wasn't healed, but my belly wasn't running the show. And even though people tried to stop me, out of friendship—Jack and the others, even the doctor—by February I was in Casablanca. I was inaugurating the club for colored American soldiers. I was singing at the Liberty Club.

I sang three songs and I wanted to dance. But my head was already dancing, my belly was burning, and I was seeing stars, there were stars all over the room.

. . . Someone was holding my hand. I was lying on a chaise longue.

"Miss Baker, please . . ."

I sat up straight.

"At your service, General!"

And that night I was in the salons of the Anfa Hotel, being received by General Clark, with all the diplomats in their suits and all the captains of the Allied army in full dress uniform: Patton, Anderson, Alexander, Cunningham. The most wonderful thing—I couldn't believe my eyes; they'd played a dirty trick on me at the Liberty Club. Was that Moulay Larbi and Si Menebhi there? The general had made an airplane available to them so they could come from Marrakesh.

My life as an artist was starting up again.

I gave all the Allied soldiers my songs, a little joy, and a little music. On the sole condition that they wouldn't offer me a fee. I was singing for my comrades in arms. I wasn't singing for money. Let them organize our transport. Let them allow us, sometimes, to eat in the mess when it's impossible to do otherwise. Nothing more.

Until the end of the hostilities in Africa and in Europe, I didn't make a single cent. This wasn't to make me feel better about myself. It was only natural that I bear the cost for the debts I'd had to run up by that time, because the French Army was the poorest of the lot—not that that stopped them, on several occasions, from saving the day for the Allies with next to nothing.

The Free French, the Français Libres, lent me to the Americans and then the English. In both cases, I remained exclusively in the service of France. Through my work with the French intelligence services, I knew the kind of propaganda politicians could be involved in, oh yes! I warned them all: "Anything that helps France is fine; I'll take part. Otherwise, no matter your reasons, we're enemies."

I admit now that in these situations, I had to pay a higher price for being so frank. Moldy bread and dubious canned food were my lot sometimes. I don't regret it.

And so I responded to Colonel Wyatt's friendly overtures for the colored soldiers, then Colonel Meyer's for the white Americans—he was General Eisenhower's colleague—then, later, the Englishman Major Dunstan's, head of the ENSA, for the armies' Entertainments National Service Association. Eventually, I stayed—not without difficulty because of our own disagreements—with the Free French forces.

Fernand Zimmer, a strange man and braver than most, who used to be the foreign trade adviser, took charge of organizing our tours as best as he could.

I had another comrade on my team: Fred Rey, my onetime dancer at the Casino de Paris. Fred Rey, who's originally from Austria, joined the French Foreign Legion in 1939. But during the landing, our authorities either forgot what he'd done for them or didn't know, because they put him in a concentration camp, and Jack had to get him out.

Before leaving for the first tour with the Americans, my wonderful friends in Marrakesh held a party for me at Si Menebhi's palace that lasted all night, like a tale from *One Thousand and One*

Nights. Moroccans wearing burnooses, Frenchmen, French-women, American officers, white and colored—I especially cared about the colored ones—were all together on the patio under the flowering vines. Flowers red like blood. Arab music moved between the marble pillars, as soft as the lights.

This is where I saw the mountain people's "blue dance." In the basin of the fountain, a jet of water was falling on the water lily leaves. In the reception room, all lit up on the other side of the patio, was Colonel Archie Roosevelt, the president's son.

My expedition with the Americans started with a series of performances at the Rialto cinema in Casablanca; the first one was in aid of the Red Cross.

A platoon of Spahis in full uniform, swords drawn, stood in a line.

At the end of the show, I sang "J'ai Deux Amours" as usual, "I Have Two Loves" . . . But there was only one—I felt it in the unbelievable applause—a single love here, for all of us: Paris.

The other performances at the Rialto—at a time when we had so little that toward the end we had nothing for lunch—raised a few hundred thousand francs. We needed to spend it as quickly as possible, for the soldiers.

And so, for a month, between Oran and Algiers, not a day went by when I didn't sing in the open air three or four times in one camp or another, in front of men standing around a little platform: a plank of wood on two cans. Didn't matter. I changed my costume in a tent. They cheered my dress that was in the colors of Paris, my Breton clogs, my Brazilian scarf, the anthems I sang to finish the show. An orchestra accompanied me, made of a few colored soldiers, volunteers.

One night, a few kilometers away from Oran—I was dressed as a "1900s cabaret dancer"—I saw a firework explode above our heads. In one second, the headlights of the trucks lighting the stage went out. The whole audience was flat on their stomachs. Me, too. German airplanes were dive-bombing us. I tried to eat a sandwich to distract myself. And what did I hear in the darkness? Someone calling me: "Miss Baker? Miss Baker?" It was a soldier crawling toward me. He was bringing me a vanilla ice cream.

Mostaganem, Blida . . . Our little caravan—three dusty vehicles with luggage on top—went from gala to gala. I tried bringing everyone together with my good mood. It wasn't always easy, with these men from all over the world and those from Africa.

In spring '43, once I'd rested in Marrakesh, we met once more with General de Gaulle's staff in Algiers at a dinner also attended by Colonel Billotte, Major de Boislambert, Lieutenant-Colonel Sémidéi, Fernand Zimmer, and Jacques Abtey.

In Algiers, supporters of de Gaulle and Giraud were grappling with everything their mission entailed: retaliation, grief, ridiculous obstacles, and, between the different bureaus, short-lived schemes, when pride was at stake, not to mention personal gain.

I'd wanted to devote myself to the French troops who were holding position from Gabès to Tripoli. But it was with the English that I was put on a bomber plane, in the month of June.

The fact I could speak English meant I could travel across Egypt and the Near East at top speed, in three weeks, alongside Major Dunstan, despite the desert winds and the occasional diplomatic incident.

I sang at the borders of Libya and Tripolitania, under the Arc de Triomphe erected by Mussolini, on a big airfield that roasted in the sun like a baking sheet. Then, from camp to camp, from airplane to airplane, to Benghazi, Tobruk, Alexandria, with the Greeks as well, Belgians, Czechs, soldiers from Israel. To Cairo, in hospitals full of the wounded from El Alamein, Mersa Matruh, Sollum, and Bir Hakeim . . . From there to Lebanon and Syria, where Monsieur Helleu, the French ambassador, and his wife kindly welcomed me to Beirut. But the things I saw and heard didn't bode well for us. The Muslims had learned the Atlantic Charter by heart, and lots of other things, too, that were being explained to them from the sidelines, that several different sides were suggesting to them at once, in an odd way. They started protesting, rising up against us, everywhere. I was surprised. But I couldn't be mistaken, no, as much as they tried to ease my worry, which I was struggling to put into words.

On July 15, when I returned, I shared the news with my colleagues. They were concerned; they spoke to the ones at the top. And Colonel Billotte asked us to leave immediately.

This time it was a propaganda tour for the Free French forces, under the banner of General de Gaulle, in support of the French Resistance groups in mainland France.

God, it's so painful to talk about. You know, when one has to take action, it's torture; it's like a woman about to give birth. It's agony. Then it's over. We forget . . . I came back from the Middle East. I had to go back to the Middle East . . . Oh, là là! I was so tired.

While we waited for Major Brousset to work things out for us and receive the mission orders, I quickly went back to Marrakesh, to Si Mohamed's guesthouse, where I would hear the muezzin's voice peacefully singing for prayers.

It wasn't long, that rest!

The jeep was fully loaded. There were three of us in front: Si Mohamed—a dear and precious colleague throughout the Muslim world, he left everything behind for this mission, even his burnoose—Jack at the wheel, and me. Two big trunks and some suitcases in the back, our corporal conductor on top. We each had a side cap, a jacket, and khaki shorts. Four soldiers on an adventure and more than sixteen thousand kilometers to cover in those outfits.

We passed through Casablanca, Rabat, Fez, Oujda, Tlemcen . . . Three days and three nights to get to Algiers. It was scorching hot. We were cooked, cramped together like dried figs. We were dying of thirst. We were covered in the dust of the convoys as we drove. But in Algiers, we received our reward.

General de Gaulle welcomed our friend Si Mohamed with all the courtesy his titles deserved.

At the Grand Théâtre, at the end of the performance, the general had his ordnance officer present me with a little gold Cross of Lorraine.

Forty-eight hours later, we were en route to Tunis. Fortunately, our luggage was following us in another car. We could breathe more easily. But our luck would soon run out. We got lost in the mountains in Kabylia, in the moonlight, between menacing mountain peaks and ravines that we couldn't see the bottom of. Then the steering broke in the car with the luggage. Then, before we got to Tunis, in the deserted zone destroyed by fighting, in the middle of a village in ruins, our jeep's engine died.

Captain Mezan, intended as a replacement for Fernand Zimmer, the leader of our group, did a good job in Tunis. Our three shows—in which a Tahitian troop took part, volunteers from the Pacific Battalion—went down very well, despite a few . . . "difficulties" . . . between the Allies. For example, under the pretext that the theater was requisitioned by English troops, the British Army's Military Police wanted to ban French soldiers from entering the theater, the very night that the performance was *for* French soldiers . . . Everything was sorted out, naturally.

I practically flew through the desert. I hadn't been there before, Monsieur Sauvage. Now we were living in it.

In Tunis we borrowed two jeeps that some soft-footed friends had repainted. I say "borrowed" . . . You understand, because the French Army didn't have equipment, or so little. So, to avoid the Military Police, who don't like people borrowing their cars without asking, we sped all the way to Tripoli at two o'clock in the morning.

Tunis to Cairo, three thousand five hundred or four thousand kilometers.

One oasis followed another, one cemetery after another, where nameless soldiers rested without flowers or wreaths. We saluted their graves. Over the graves in Saoura, the Gaullists' cemetery, we saw a big wooden Cross of Lorraine: planks put up among the skinny cypress trees.

And we drank from the oases' little streams. And at night, the stars were fat like tears.

One hundred kilometers outside Tripoli, Captain Mezan left us. We were safe here. Our mission lay ahead of us.

"Goodbye, Josephine, see you in Paris!"

How sad! He never saw France again, Captain Mezan. He was killed in Italy.

✦ ✦ ✦

The desert isn't empty. It has an extraordinary, mysterious life. The wind speaks; it rolls like a drum. And the mirages are like Sirens from the past, beautiful men and women, so beautiful.

At night, we'd sleep where we could on the ground. And the shadows would rise, shapes coming toward us slowly, as if to surround us, lurking in the desert, robbing dead bodies, stealing lifeless scrap metal, broken airplanes, burned and abandoned cars, gutted tanks, little cannons like black fingers pointed at the sky or ridiculously out-of-place toys. And other shadows moved, like stains on the white sand. Shadows that barked and moaned and howled. Jackals, hyenas, which also came to sniff at the battle ruins, to dig up the dead.

We had to sleep in our coats while one of us kept watch.

We stayed in Alexandria for four days.

Prince Mohamed Ali told us that France still had a big role to play in the Middle East.

"France must take part in the political progress of the Arab peoples."

He said again: "Tell General de Gaulle that we need, that we will always need France in the Middle East. Independence is desirable . . . When one can be sure of one's own independence. The mosaic of the Arab peoples is not set in stone. It is unstable. And we need stability and certainties; we need guides."

In Cairo, we made plans, but first we had to rush to Lebanon, to Beirut, where I gave up my little gold Cross of Lorraine so it could be sold at auction: three hundred and fifty thousand francs for the Resistance . . . To Damascus, the white, flat city hanging off the mountainside in halos of blue mist . . . To Jerusalem, where they have the most beautiful hotel in the world, the King David, all in marble. And the light that the good Lord gave that city is truly miraculous. Nothing is lost to the eye, everything stands out, clear, outlined in that light . . . To Jericho . . . Other places, too. And Si Mohamed Menebhi was talking to the Arabs. Jack was talking to the Arabs. But the Arab Union slogans that were developing at the time, secretly supported by the English, were also making inroads.

When we got back to Judaea—where the last thing I saw was Mary Magdalene the sinner's house, in a little village—anti-French demonstrations were taking place in Cairo. We, however, put on a big show that was attended by Peter I, King of Yugoslavia, and His Majesty King Farouk along with several of his ministers.

On November 15, 1943, we went back from Alexandria to Algiers across the desert. It was cold.

I pulled my side cap down over my ears and wrapped myself up in the big Cross of Lorraine flag that the nuns had lovingly stitched and embroidered; it was my only piece of scenery, the only backdrop on all the stages in all the places I stopped in.

For three years, year-ends were horrible for me. December 1943, oh, là là! In January 1944, I was in Marrakesh again, in Marrakesh Hospital. The doctors were slicing up my belly once more . . . I was crawling back from the furthest I'd ever been. But my loyal friends were there. And three hundred poor people, blind people, crippled people, to whom Si Mohamed Menebhi had given out bread, were praying to Allah night and day under my windows so I'd get better. And I did get better.

In April, I sang, at the request of General Béthouart—the commander in chief of the local French forces—for a party in honor of the air force, in Algiers.

Do you know that I cost the French Air Force an aircraft? Yes: I was shipwrecked in a Seagull off the coast of Corsica. No luck for me. Seagulls and I, we don't get on.

General Bouscat—I owe it to him for my appointment as a second lieutenant; I spent a wonderful few days at his place while I was recovering—made me take a Seagull to reach Morocco. In the middle of a storm above Taza, we were shaken about so much that we had to go back to Meknes. Warning number one.

And there it was, another Seagull waiting for me at the Boufarik airfield, near Algiers. That morning, having already landed in Normandy, the Allies were now entering Bayeux. We'd just found out. The wind was filled with joy. The sky was blue, pure blue. We left. I was going to do a brief tour in Corsica, with Zimmer, Jack, and René Guérin.

The cabin was filled with sunlight. Below us, the mountains of Kabylia were scattering like sheep. Then the sea, pure blue as well. The airplane was rumbling quietly when one of the propellers, all of a sudden . . . "Wait a second, it's not turning as fast. It's stopping. It's not moving at all." But we kept going.

"The left-hand engine's screwed, but the other one will manage," the pilot said. "I promised to drop you off in Ajaccio; you'll be there in ten minutes."

But the Seagull was losing more and more height. The radio operator was tapping frantically at his keypad. The airplane was pitching. It was pitching more and more. And in front of us was Corsica—that is, a mountain, an enormous, sheer, rising wall.

"We'll never clear it," said Zimmer.

Next to me, Guérin was looking out a window. Jack was watching the pilot. When we saw the great granite wall looming over us—it was rushing toward us so quickly—we closed our eyes . . .

Nothing. The Seagull had leaped over it. It went down again; the second engine was choking, full of oil. We were no more than one or two hundred meters above water, right in the middle of a huge bay.

The pilot shouted, "Brace yourselves . . . Brace yourselves!"

His rounded back, enormous to our eyes; his arms, his elbows wide, splayed out, his clenched hands . . . That was all. We fell.

We fell. We were gutted like fish. Then a sudden jolt, a horrible punch in the nose for everyone. An explosion of wood, an explosion of water—water like milk—a gigantic spray of water.

On the beach, some colored men, naked, riflemen, were bathing. They're the ones who saved us. They were swimming like seals.

General Bouscat sent us another airplane.

I warned Monsieur Luizet, head of the local police: "If it's a Seagull, I'm out of here."

But it was a Glenn Martin. It was under orders to take us first to the base in Cagliari. It was the day before a big battle. I sang there one last time before returning to France with my back pressed against a mast flying the Cross of Lorraine flag, among masses of airplanes ready to take off with their bombs under the wings, shining in the moonlight.

I hadn't seen France for four years. As soon as Marseille was liberated, I asked to be repatriated. I wanted to serve in France with French people. I was put on one of the first lists. We all gathered, all the air force girls, in a convent for nuns near Algiers, in Guyotville. A military train took us—me and my whole section, in field uniform, bags on our backs, flasks and haversacks at our sides—to board a "Liberty ship" at the port in Mers El-Kébir.

At the dock, an officer arrived to inspect us. No animals allowed on board.

"But what about Mitraillette?"

Mitraillette was a little dog, the section's lucky mascot.

I'd named him Mitraillette because he would pee all the time; short, sharp splashes like a machine gun, rat-tat-tat, five, six drops with his leg in the air.

All my other animals had disappeared in Africa. I didn't want to leave Mitraillette there. So he was secretly passed from bag to bag until he got to a man working in the storeroom, who took care of him.

And I landed in Marseille with Mitraillette.

SECRETS FROM THE BOUDOIR

Jo and Jo

don't really like that title, Monsieur Sauvage, nor boudoirs themselves. What a strange word. It has a stale aftertaste. It smells like showing off, people showing off, that word, don't you think? As for telling you whether I prefer a man to have a beauty mark on his right shoulder or the left side of his chest; which techniques I like or don't like or that excite me in some way, you can wait as long as you like.

Even if I were a penniless old woman, like I was as a child, I would never use memories of my heart and of my nights, never, to get back in the spotlight, to sell newsprint about myself—stories that are even more unfortunate, you know, for being uninteresting, inelegant, and not very decent, oh, no! Despite some unhappy or unthinking artists, who are quite incapable of writing themselves, sometimes making them seem so.

It's true, perhaps, that I have a lot of the little colored girl in the way I am and the way I understand things. People sure love to say it. But now they criticize me for putting clothes on, for hiding myself . . . Oh well. Let me be as modest as a little savage. In life, it's the only personal treasure we can keep, or else a sorrow that's a pointless addition to other people's pain, don't you think? And for me, secrets—I know how to keep them—really are secrets.

Plus, quite simply, I've always been in love. An artist, a man or a woman, who doesn't have a sense of seduction, the gift of love, faith in the mysterious rendezvous, is not an *artist*. Art, you know, is seduction, passion, the pursuit of life in its most inspiring, most beautiful, sweetest things. My first love was my mother . . . then my father . . . and finally my brother, who runs a garage in St. Louis.

My mother never saw me on a stage until 1949. She was so emotional—it was a Thursday, April 28—that her nose bled throughout the entire show at the Folies. She had two little balls of cotton wool in her nostrils. She couldn't believe she was my mama, that she'd found her daughter. But I had a lovely house set up for her in the Dordogne, near Les Milandes, for her and my sister. Before coming to France, both of them had their teeth pulled out—they still had good ones—so they could have a brand-new set of pretty false teeth with blue gums fitted, as is the fashion for colored people in America. They wanted to impress the Frenchmen. Unfortunately, Mama's new teeth hurt. She was heartbroken, was Mama! She couldn't laugh like she wanted to. But now she's so happy with us, my poor dear Mama.

When I was little, actually, my first love was a little white boy. He was handsome . . . A little redhead with freckles all over his skin, freckles are delightful! I was in awe. I didn't dare speak to him. I often saw him. I'd make big eyes at him like this, rolling them around, which must have frightened him.

One day, I deliberately dropped my photograph in front of him so he would talk to me. He picked it up and he told me to keep it. I felt ashamed. I ran away.

Later on, we played together. I would say to him: "Let's play being in love!" I'd look at his freckles, one by one, up close. He'd stroke my hair; I have the coarsest hair that's ever been on a head. I buried my head between my shoulders. But he said I was the prettiest in the world. And I cried, I was so happy. I waited. He didn't kiss me, that little redhead. He didn't know. He was too little. But I loved him—my God, how I loved him!

Maybe it's a dream or the story from a film, I don't remember.

Life, when you think about it later, is a series of images that surprise you, as if they were of someone else, often; a film in your heart, in your head. It doesn't always match up. And then work distracts you. It changes you in its own way. It carries you away. There are big empty spaces where nothing happens anymore, just shadows scattered through your memory, some useful, some not, silent shadows, far away, so faint. You've got to look twice to recognize them. Everyday work has driven them away. They have no substance anymore, almost no voice . . . Entire years. And others, on the contrary, are still there, present.

From 1926 to 1935, my manager was Pepito Abatino. He looked like Adolphe Menjou, only thinner. He had the manners of a diplomat, but energetic. He was from Italy, very active, maybe too much. He had been unwell. He really championed me when I still didn't know how to manage contracts, documents, business proposals I received, traps they hand out to you with a smile and chocolate boxes bigger than suitcases. For nine years, which were among the most difficult for my work, in France, he devoted himself to my interests as if they were his own.

He dreamed for me, with me, of all the best that life could bring. He even imagined I could be a novelist. I told him a few stories about the lives of white and colored people in America. And so he wrote *Mon Sang dans Tes Veines*—"My Blood in Your Veins"—under my name.

It's the true adventure of Joan, a little colored friend. I wrote the preface myself. Read a little bit, I insist . . .

This poor Joan, whose story you are going to read, is somebody I knew . . . Actually, no: it's not her that I knew, but dozens of Joans, little girls from St. Louis who were all colored. Was it because we lived in an area full of smoky factories?

Summer in Louisiana was so sweltering that one was surprised not to see palm trees in the street. We would escape to the river; on the docks, near the coal boats, longshoremen who were black with soot and tattoos were getting ready for winter in the middle of summer. But they turned white again once they emerged from the waters of the river.

"You see! What's in a color anyway?" Joan would say to me . . . [14]

A novelist . . . Imagine me sitting, night and day, pen in my hand. Oh, no! God knows I've had other pens. The reputation they brought me has damaged me enough. But I enjoyed trying, with this sort of novel developed by Pepito, to defend the cause of colored children once more, in a different way, and to gaze on the little lost face of a childhood friend. She was intelligent and so tormented, was Joan, so timid, like a bird, a really small one that had fallen into the coal and had become unrecognizable but who just couldn't understand why everyone looked down on her.

I used to reassure her in those days. My own fortune had given me tri-colored blood. Mama was colored. Papa was white. Aunt Elvira was an Indian. It's true, I haven't confessed everything to you yet. There's Indian blood in my family, too. Joan remembered. I was well placed, you see, to talk about that great drama that shakes everyone up: the mixing of blood.

Mon sang dans tes veines is the story of a blood transfusion.

One day, Joan and I found a colored Virgin Mary in a chapel, a niche with no flowers, no light, abandoned.

For us, little girls from the street, it was a revelation of love, I swear, something life-changing, as if we'd opened the enchanted doors to the greatest love of all.

A colored Virgin Mary, sweet and beautiful, to smile on us, console us, protect us . . .

Joan . . . What became of her? As for me, some white men married me.

Poor Pepito died from a stomach ulcer. We said Mass for him at Saint Philippe du Roule, here in Paris. Now I want him buried near me. The dead are still family. He'll be moved to the Château des Milandes, near the little chapel, where my last marriage was blessed. Dear Pepito from my early days.

In 1936, Monsieur Jean Lion married me before the mayor of Crèvecoeur-le-Grand.

Jean was a young industrialist, a Jew.

The mayor, who was Monsieur Jammy Schmidt, read us some passages from the law. Then he made a lovely speech for us; a smile beyond the call of duty; compliments. Jean was delighted. So was I, no less so.

But sadly! We separated, three years later. Then we divorced. The judge said: "In conclusion, here is a couple who never saw each other. They didn't have time to spend with each other . . ."

He was right. And there was no other reason. I'd come back from the cabaret at around five or six in the morning. An hour later, Jean would leave for his office. I'd sleep late into the afternoon. In the evening, I would dine in a hurry to go to the show. Often, Jean hadn't got back yet. I understood that this was no way to live. Not to mention the trips I had to make, the tours outside Paris or abroad . . . Can an artist give up the stage? Every night, an artist's family, the real one despite everything, their big family, is their audience.

But Jean's mother is still my Mama Lion. My love for her hasn't changed; she welcomed me so warmly. She said I was the only woman who could put up with her son. Unfortunately, I can't say he was the only man who could put up with me—with the person my profession forces me to be.

But we're still good friends.

After our divorce, Jean asked me to marry him again. But it couldn't be done. Life decided otherwise.

I'd have preferred never to have divorced. But I'm not cut out for fantasies, the small delusions of luck.

Jean came to see me in Morocco, where Captain Abtey was overseeing my life as a soldier. I could help him because of my position. I was very happy about that. Thanks to the papers I could obtain, he and his family had the option to go to Brazil during the occupation.

When I got back to France, I met Jo Bouillon through the Théâtre aux Armées, the army theater, after Paris was liberated. At the time, he was conducting his orchestra at the Boeuf sur le Toit music hall.

He generously agreed to join me. We worked together, for the soldiers, in difficult conditions. I got to know him while we were rushing from post to post behind the Armée de la Victoire. Our love was born to the sound of violins, in the middle of the ruins, on makeshift stages.

Even more generously after that, Jo gave up part of his career to devote himself to mine, to some shared ventures. And we were married at the Château des Milandes in Castelnaud-Fayrac on June 3, 1947, my birthday.

Oh, what a wonderful wedding!

The path that goes from the château to the chapel, and the whole interior of the chapel, was covered in petals strewn over a beautiful carpet of leaves. The local children stood guard over the petals so no one would walk on them before the service.

But that morning, we found we didn't have an organ. The nearest one was too big to fit inside the chapel at the château. But we couldn't get married without music: a singer and an orchestra conductor? Impossible! Consider that the whole Bouillon family is a family of musicians. Papa Bouillon in Montpellier, his three sons all with first-prize diplomas from the Conservatoire de Paris:

Gabriel, now a teacher, who took over from his own teacher at the Conservatoire; Georges, first solo violin in the Pasdeloup Orchestra; and Joseph, the youngest, that's Jo . . . Joseph and Josephine, now Jo and Jo. Papa Bouillon received the prestigious Cross of the Legion of Honor thanks to his three sons. So, we had to have church music. We couldn't get married without the sound of an organ.

Jo left at dawn, in shorts, in his car, to scout around the area. He found a pretty little harmonium in Domme. The parish priest of Domme, eighty years old, said: "I would really like to lend it to you, but I can't help you transport it." So, the village butcher came.

And luckily there was an enormous truck that had brought the marble pillars over from my old house in Le Vésinet.

The owner of the truck said: "Don't worry. This is the truck that the Germans made me use to remove all the statues in Paris. I can handle a harmonium."

And so we had music.

Plus, Georges, Jo's brother, played us a violin piece composed by Pierre Guillermin for the occasion.

And in the evening, the local people made Jo a lovely pepper soup, as was the custom. It warms up the groom, you see, it's wonderful. Jo ate it all.

Five days later, we took off from Orly to America by airplane.

Meanwhile, I came across some of General de Gaulle's good and loyal colleagues. I said to them: "My opinion—rather, my impression—doesn't really matter, but I feel, I think, I'm sure that you'd like to work toward freeing Marshal Pétain. There's a politics above politics, isn't there? Whatever his weaknesses, the tragedy of this great and venerable soldier hides one last secret: the opportunity for you to rediscover, in France, a coming together of all men of goodwill, I believe."

Some said yes. Others said no—firmly, too much. Then I left!

I'll tell you what we did in America, but first, the beautiful story with Jo, before our marriage.

When I landed in Marseille with Mitraillette in '44, I immediately went to see General Chadebec de Lavalade, who was commanding the Fifteenth Military Region.

The Théâtre aux Armées was no more, nor was any service or organization to help casualties, even though they needed—really needed—help, and fast.

The general tasked me with organizing a group that would first perform in the Riviera and then follow the military operations as they progressed toward the east. I needed an orchestra. I didn't know whom to ask. Monsieur Yves Bonnat, who was in charge of purging the French music halls of suspected collaborators, suggested I get in contact with Monsieur Jo Bouillon. Paris had been liberated for a few weeks; Jo was playing at the Boeuf sur le Toit.

Equipped with my mission, I was in Paris, in October, for twenty-four hours. Monsieur Bouillon wasn't at home or at the Boeuf. He was rehearsing with his radio orchestra. I found him in the studio with his musicians. It was interesting. I'd never watched work like theirs. It was quite something. Not a minute to lose. But no way to talk . . . Plus, I was in uniform; we weren't allowed at cabaret shows. No way to go and explain myself at the Boeuf sur le Toit, either . . .

I left a little note with Jo, inviting him to an emergency meeting at two in the morning at my house. I was living on Boulevard de Dixmude, and I had an airplane to catch at six.

Jo woke me at two in the morning. I'd left the doors open. I received him as I was, my head wrapped in scarves because I get cold at night and I like to sleep with a thirty-six-layer turban that makes my little head disappear. Which really shocked Jo, to see me in private for the first time like this.

He probably thought I had a business proposal for him. I immediately set him straight. This was no business matter. I was asking him to leave everything behind: the Boeuf, the radio, his contracts, as quickly as possible, and to join me . . . for no money . . . for an unknown length of time. I was simply accepting my responsibilities. It was for him to accept his. He was speechless, sweet Jo. He must have thought I was dreaming. I may have had a big head, but his eyes were all round. For an hour and a quarter I quietly explained to him what was on offer, and he was sold. In principle, he was willing, but he asked for a little time to let his musicians know.

He's wonderful, is Jo, and he's good. I love that. Eight days later, with his twenty-five musicians, we made our debut in Marseille for the city's victims. Bordas was one of us, too, even though her mother was very unwell at the time. A top lady, Marcelle Bordas, a beautiful artist, and a kind-hearted woman. Jean Tranchant was also there.

The second part of the show was mine. That's when I thought up my little costume-change trick, ten dresses one after the other. There was a reason behind it. We needed to show support for the couturiers who were taking part in the gala.

From Marseille we did the whole of the Riviera, as far as Monte Carlo, passing through Toulon, Cannes, and Nice. The tour brought in two million for the victims' emergency fund.

On the way back up to Paris, we picked up a dozen little Resistance fighters, kids no more than twelve years old who were roaming the countryside and wanted to join the army, poor little heroes. Apart from that, only sad things, awful things. In Besançon, in the hospital and the health facilities, I saw more than two hundred young people with their feet cut off . . . They had been blown up by mines that the Germans had planted behind them as they retreated.

✦ ✦ ✦

Now we were working for the First Army, on their heels, so to speak, but specially assigned to the African commando units. I had safe-conducts, like a diplomat; a military mission order, undated, permanent. We performed and sang along the way, occasionally on the side of the street, with only a guitar as accompaniment, or in a barn by the light of a few oil lamps. Jo made do, always smiling, friendly, ready to round up his people. We were divided up between different messes, the musicians here, Jo somewhere else, me with the officers. The rations were sparse. Sometimes, some men did without for our sake. We would sing for them, even in the snow, even in the mud.

And who wouldn't have followed Colonel Bouvet?

It was snowing in Belfort; we were there during the attacks to liberate Alsace. I asked them to let me go to the front line, twenty kilometers away, in the pocket or at a bridgehead—is that what you say? Major Ferragi took me in a jeep. Then we were on foot, one group at a time. And the shells were exploding across the snow.

On rest days, as the soldiers advanced, we and the Resistance fighters reopened the theaters in every city: Mulhouse, Nancy, Colmar . . . In Strasbourg, it was while the Germans were counterattacking. We were part of the first crossing over the Rhine. There was a big expedition into German lines. When they got back, we put on a show for the commando units; each one of us, to show our admiration, wanted to surpass ourselves. In comparison, you know, it wasn't much; at least it was with our whole heart.

And everywhere, I looked for colored soldiers. The poor Senegalese! I saw so many with frozen feet! One day, in the mountains, on the other side of Konstanz, one of them gave me a little doe. It was his baby, maybe the only thing he loved that he still had in this world, you understand? I didn't want to take it. He forced me to take the little creature; he was crying.

On January 3, 1945, we were in Berlin. The Allies were putting on their first gala; the four generals were the guests of honor.[15] Four groups of artists, English, French, Russian, and American, featured in the program. I had the honor of representing France with Jo Bouillon and Colette Mars. Don't forget Colette Mars, a truly great comrade, so lovely, so modest. But she was the daughter of a general, you know, General Huot. And the Bishop of Algiers comes from their family, too.

For this gala, the French had a budget of thirty thousand francs in all. Didn't matter. The artists and musicians refused to be paid.

We were competing in another way, trying to appear better than each other. Money never made anyone shine.

It was held in the courthouse, in the middle of ruins and rats. Berlin—what a dreadful impression it made! I didn't recognize the avenues, or the parks, or the monuments. There were none left. Nothing but holes, rubble, and iron girders. The courthouse had also been hit. It was lit up by big spotlights. It looked like each piece was burning, what was left of it. It was on fire. It was glowing.

The Americans, the MPIs, acted as stewards, with white gloves. Their hands looked like they'd caught fire, too, in the spotlights.

Inside the courthouse there were four buffets. But we didn't have the stomach to touch any of them. There were four intermissions. So many salutes, smiles, colors, medals; so much bowing. Stars and stripes, arm in arm. I closed the show. Jo was magnificent; his musicians were wonderful. I saw everyone's hands clapping. But I said to myself: "No, Josephine, it's not for you, it's for the country that, twenty years ago, adopted a little colored dancer whose only wish was to escape, to try and do well, to always do better, if luck would allow it."

We stayed in Berlin for ten days.

The gala, all that fuss for the generals, the officers, the divisions, it was perfect, but what about the soldiers?

For them—who deserved even more, you know—we found a little cinema in the French quarter. And we performed there, every day, around the clock, from ten in the morning to eleven at night. Every two hours: a performance, curtain, next show. The orchestra didn't stop. Jo kept going like a windmill. We exhausted the whole repertoire. The soldiers came as they pleased, one hundred and fifty for two cents each. And you know what they did, the soldiers? They gave us piles, kilos, hundreds of kilos of German certificates of good conduct that they'd found in the basements of the Reichstag, under the rubble . . . Proof that we'd be Aryans, and good ones, forever!

And you know who served me in my house? A very stylish butler, I swear to you: the former police chief of Potsdam.

We stopped in a lot of devastated, unrecognizable cities in Germany: Karlsruhe, Stuttgart, Hamburg . . . Hamburg, a desert. Mountains of rubble kilometers long. Along the docks, there were hundreds, thousands, of bells, stolen from countries all over Europe. Bells that used to ring for the Angelus, in another time, throughout the small villages.

In Sigmaringen, I was welcomed by General de Monsabert, one of the kindest, most cheerful, serious, and direct of men, a great leader. A man of Africa, you know? He had a guard of Goumiers. Everyone admired him and loved him. I sat to his right in the château's trophy room. A lavish reception room in marble from the Hohenzollern family. I was certainly the first colored woman allowed in this throne room where those blind butchers who fed Hitler's madness had mercilessly discussed their racist policies. And there I was, shy—imagine—but proud, standing with France, alongside five generals with healthy appetites.

At night I would sleep in a little chalet with a fantastic view, frozen. Was it a dream? I wondered. I still wonder . . .

And then, peace.

Now it was time to work, to win back the audience from the days before the war. I left for Scandinavia, for Finland, beautiful lands with unmistakable goodwill. With Jo.

The Scandinavians had thought I was dead. The news had spread a long time ago while I was in the clinics in Morocco. Everywhere else I appeared after the war, people had a hard time recognizing me. There was even a great deal of discussion about me in Switzerland, even in the newspapers. Some of them were sure: No, that's not Josephine. That's a double, a stand-in. This one is thinner. She might be rather good but she doesn't have Josephine's figure; she's too thin. Others would reply: We might be wrong about her body, but our Josephine had a quiet, cooing voice, and this one, listen, she's a trained singer; she has a stronger voice, much clearer.

You know what it's like, Monsieur Sauvage. When people think you're dead, you speak up. But people always struggle to recognize the living. People thought that France, too, was dead. That didn't stop her from being in concert.

In Helsinki, for two weeks, five hundred people waited at the hotel doors from morning till night, to give you an idea. I performed in such very different places there, for all kinds of audiences, from the National Theater to the People's House. And I got so many gifts that I made a special place in my memory for Finland.

I came back with six puppies, not all for me, but I hid them under my coat because the customs officers go easy on me. The puppies' mother was a dog that a Frenchman had left in the care of the consul of France, before leaving for the war. So it was only fair, you see, to bring the children back for the family. I kept one pretty puppy, Flicka. She's at Les Milandes; a piece of Finland in the Dordogne.

Finally, Europe stopped doubting that I was alive and well. And I was able to take care of the sorry people of Paris. There were still so many of them. I went, myself, to Les Halles and to La Villette, to buy meat—good pieces—and vegetables for "Le pot-au-feu des vieux," to feed the elderly, a cause that I would never have enough time and money for. The elderly, the poor, these days they're nearly all neglected, left behind. People will never do enough to make sure they can keep living, despite everything.

Life . . . Who knows how it will turn out? Mine, in '46, was full of turmoil, ups, downs, more downs than ups. My marriage wasn't completely fixed. We had to keep reconsidering it, get past the emotions. Jo went to Switzerland, I went to Morocco. I did one last tour in North Africa to raise money for the air force support services.

When I returned, it was to be admitted to the Ambroise Paré Hospital. It seemed I wasn't destined to come out again—or if I did, then it would be to the cemetery, like Raimu a few weeks before. I was alone in Paris . . . But the night they thought I was as good as gone—after a useless operation—Jo rushed over from Geneva and Jacques Abtey from Morocco; they were there, both of them, at my bedside. My belly was open, burned by the surgical products. At two in the morning, they gave up whatever treatment I was on. But love and friendship don't give up. In the end, they always win. Jo and Jack called for a transfusion. They roamed the hospitals and pharmacies to get hold of a rather rare medicine; I can't remember its name . . . Wait: Subtosan, an ampoule of Subtosan. Anyway, thanks to that medicine and the transfusion, at seven in the morning I was saved, in spite of the doctor. But I wasn't *cured*.

July, August, September . . . On my little bed in the Ambroise Paré, Monsieur Jean Pierre-Bloch and Colonel de Boissoudy presented me with a Medal of the Resistance. Because I had a hard life, probably—for when I think about it all now, I don't think I did anything extraordinary to deserve this honor. Everything was as it had to be, quite simply.

All through autumn '46, I rested at Les Milandes, with my animals and my fields. Good decision. On December 30, I was in Paris. The next morning, at nine o'clock, I was on Rue Georges Bizet; at eleven thirty I was on the operating table for a surgery that would last three and a half hours. Do you know, Marcel, what they told me a little later? That since 1940, they'd opened my belly five times . . . They'd looked inside. But practically none of these specialists, no one, had dared to do anything. They were scared. They stitched me back up and left me to the grace of God. Maybe they did the right thing, since Providence kept me for Doctor Thiroloix and Doctor Funck-Brentano. I owe my life to them; they finally made me myself again.

Thank you, Docteur Thiroloix! Thank you, Docteur Funck-Brentano! Those words aren't enough, but anything more wouldn't be enough, either.

On January 21, 1947, I left the hospital.

My wedding date with Jo was set. I went back to Les Milandes. Jo left for South America in March. He needed to organize a tour that we'd planned as a honeymoon. Unfortunately, after a month and a half, no contract! Even over there they wondered how Josephine Baker could be alive; the directors who did believe I was living thought I must have become one hundred years old—in less than ten years, apparently.

Jo wrote me letters. He was so upset, ready to come home empty-handed, when, at the last minute, Hugo del Carril, a singer and actor, the great star who played Carlos Gardel in the cinema, offered to help us. He organized everything with such kindness—not without some friendly sass as well.

And voilà. Less than a week after our wedding, at eleven at night, Jo and Jo were flying to South America.

Our departure was not without incident.

One hundred and fifty kilometers away from Orly, our transatlantic airplane had to turn around. One of the engines wasn't running properly. I remembered my adventures in the Seagull off the coast of Corsica. This swim in the air was quite enough for me now. I wanted to forget flying and take the boat.

Jo was tearing his hair out . . . Couldn't be late . . . Hugo del Carril had gone to so much trouble, was vouching for us . . .

Very well. At midnight, we got back in the airplane.

———

We had a contract for two weeks in Buenos Aires. We stayed there for three and a half months, at the Politeama. A marvelous artistic director. A wonderful hotel, the Alvear Palace. Jo put together an orchestra with local musicians, all excellent; they all wanted to speak French. And after the Politeama, I would sing in a marvelous nightclub, the Golden Gate.

We were such a success that the French ambassador, Count d'Ormesson, asked us to put on a show for him at the embassy. Even better that Jo's brother, Gabriel Bouillon, had joined us with his violin. His classical recitals were drawing in big crowds.

Jo, Gabriel, and I performed in fifteen cities in Argentina before going to Mendoza to cross the Andes . . . Eighteen hours of railway for only one hundred and twenty kilometers. We crossed the range, thirty-six hundred meters high. Even though the train had a big engine on each end, it kept running out of steam, kept stopping on the tracks. What do you know! Believe it or not, there on the tracks, there were railway workers asking me for I don't know how many photographs and autographs . . . At thirty-six hundred meters high, you see, in the Andes . . . I was happy.

In Chile—President Gabriel González Videla was a writer, an old Parisian; he kindly paid us a visit; we talked about the banks of the Seine and Rue de la Paix—we met General de Lattre de Tassigny, a very stylish general, at our ambassador the Count de Dampierre's residence.

And then . . . And then . . . So many memories have slipped away . . . Like others from the past . . . Peru, Ecuador, Mexico . . . In each country, Jo put together a new orchestra, studied the folklore, adapted it, had fun, delighted everybody. But in Mexico, our musicians sang along to "Sous les Ponts de Paris," "Under the

Bridges of Paris." I tell you, that, too, was marvelous. The president held a reception in our honor. Jo gave him the manuscript for one of the songs, in a pretty box. In return, the president, Mr. Miguel Alemán—don't forget his name—gave me an ancient ring, wonderful, heavy and beautifully crafted. Maybe a magic ring. Either way, it brought us good luck.

But what I have to tell you now, about North America, is not so amusing.

No Jews, no dogs, no niggers . . .

Voilà. That's what they boil down to, Americans, in their country, along with the atomic bomb, the portable refrigerator, and chewing gum. *No Jews, no dogs, no niggers . . .* No matter what they say abroad, this is the slogan that far too many of them would have liked to see displayed as an order on all the walls of all the houses in all their states, in the North and the South, despite the differences in their laws and the slight differences in attitudes, too, between people in the North and the South. But there's a long way between propaganda initiatives and their actual results . . .

No Jews, no dogs, no niggers . . . In 1948, after the war and so much unprecedented atrocity, after so much misery, Marcel; it's heartbreaking. And I'm furious.

Tell me, what have we achieved? I wanted to serve in the war as best I could, against the Germans, because of their race policy. And that policy, I found it again, more insidious, more hideous, perhaps, among the people who claimed to fight against it. Oh! I know one shouldn't be dramatic. I know there are extenuating circumstances, that there are some well-meaning souls there. The

Americans have it all, the best and the worst and a great deal of thoughtlessness.

In this country of self-made men, Rockefeller, who started making his fortune one cent at a time by selling newspapers, is still the great example, the model of inspiration for everyone.

In this country of self-made men, any work is good if it's honest and earns money. That means anything in life is possible because one isn't afraid to get one's hands dirty. That's good, very good. It makes people work. But when we harden our hearts little by little for the sake of success, money, strength, vanity, we kill our souls. We stop listening to our hearts. Now it's the world of big Rockefellers, little Rockefellers, where we get used to wealth, also the world of all those who say "Bravo!" anytime a Rockefeller does anything eccentric, because he's the great example; now this world becomes a world of lost people. Nothing but money counts.

And yet, they are . . . Communist sympathizers, in their own way, in America. Look at them during a holiday. They all have the same funny little straw or paper hat on their head, with the same accessories, all the same clothes, the same shoes. For hours and hours they all march to music that's the same everywhere, churned out in the same way. And they all have the same sandwich in their hand, the same little cone of popcorn. They all drink the same lemonade, only the color changes, the same everywhere, two or three colors. And big businesses never lose their selling rights, even during holidays. Everything one price, a one-way street.

Americans don't have time to think. They work, study, manufacture, and have fun on command. No, they don't have time to think. That's much too difficult. They start their lives running and don't stop. They let life carry them along. But all these grandchildren of old Europe, they come back to Europe wearing beautiful, fabulous ties, to sing the praises of self-made men, to really impress their cousins in old Europe—all the better to string them along, too, don't you think?—in the name of this good old Rockefeller who used to live over there in that famous neighborhood of American aristocrats where you also find nobles from old Europe who, at the end of the day, needed money more than nobility just like everyone else.

As for the Jews, the Negroes, the Chinese . . .

It also seems, perhaps, that certain problems are blamed on these races because a master race—sometimes one, sometimes another—wants to keep them under their thumb. Yes, I know. And on the other hand, you know I don't like anything in life that's melodramatic. But I'm not an "Uncle Tom," like us colored people say about folk who'll go down on their knees, flat on their stomachs, who'll say nothing, who'll make the best out of anything, who fool around, who agree—because they're so terribly exhausted—to be and always be good, well-behaved, feeble Negroes. Oh, no! Now, I've already told you, I'm not a novelist, I find it hard to make things up; I don't know how to lie. But I had the chance to be a sort of journalist, to lead an inquiry and to write. I wrote some notes and sent a few articles on this subject to Roger Féral, who published them in the newspaper *France-Soir*. Here they are. Take them. Then I'll tell you more, because this is only one part of the truth.

✦ ✦ ✦

Things must have changed in the United States! The war, which mixed together peoples and races, which saw white and colored people fighting side by side, must have broken down barriers and eradicated "color" prejudices . . . That is what I was thinking as I made my way back to North America after twelve years of absence. We had just spent a good few months in South America, my husband, Jo Bouillon, and I, where we had given hundreds of performances. Our airplane was taking us from Mexico to Chicago.

Our stay in Chicago—without the slightest incident—was about to come to an end. We asked some friends to reserve an apartment in a nice hotel in New York under the name of Mr. and Mrs. Jo Bouillon.

It was upon arriving in New York that the trouble began.

"You can stay, but . . ."

No sooner had we settled in than the hotel management asked to speak to my husband:

"Do you intend to stay for long, Mr. Bouillon?"

"I have reserved the apartment for a month."

"Very sorry . . . We've made a mistake. Your apartment is only available today . . . Tomorrow it's reserved . . ."

Jo understood immediately.

"Is this because my wife is a colored woman?"

The evil word had been released!

It's unfortunate, but that's how it is . . .

The people from the South, in the United States, still do not want to admit that colored people are people like any other (only colored Americans, however). They wouldn't stay five minutes in a hotel that would allow a mixed couple (although legally married) to share a room . . .

We received the same excuses throughout the day in the dozen hotels where we tried to find accommodation, Jo and I. We weren't fooled.

Nowhere did they dare to tell us clearly: "No. No rooms here for colored women!"

The law is clear: refusals on racial grounds are forbidden. Because in this great democratic country—officially, legally—a colored person is worth as much as a white person. They have the same rights as each other. But the law is one thing, prejudices are another . . . And proper business, which consists in not angering rich clients from the South, is a third.

We had finally found two comfortable rooms at the Gladstone Hotel on Park Avenue. Things were fine. I was beginning to forget the ill treatment that I had been subjected to when, on the third day, the farce began again:

"Very sorry, Mr. Bouillon . . . Someone else has reserved your rooms tomorrow."

Furious, Jo replied:

"I am also very sorry, *but we shall not leave."*

I should mention that, in the meantime, we had told the great colored actor Canada Lee, the darling of Broadway, about our ordeal. Canada Lee—like Lena Horne, like all the colored stars, like all the other colored people—had right of residence in the North of the United States, where racial prejudices tended to disappear, provided that everyone stayed in their place.

He promised to take measures for us. He went to see Mr. O'Dwyer, the mayor of New York.

"Tell Mr. Bouillon and Miss Baker," the mayor replied, "that the law stands behind them. If anyone wants to make them leave their hotel, they must let me know; I will strongly intervene."

Strengthened by these words, Jo refused to move.

The management did not ask again.

That evening, as usual, we were served dinner in our apartment.

We were brought what we had ordered, but without plates or cutlery . . . No tablecloth, no napkins.

"What's going on?" I asked.

"Very sorry . . . We're a little short on supplies at the moment."

When we rang the call bell, no one came.

The next day, the beds were not made, the telephone was no longer working . . . Understood. We were not being forced to leave, but . . . but they would make our lives unbearable so that we would not stay. At that point, I decided to leave—not only the hotel, but to leave New York, a northern city, to go and find out what was happening in the South, where racial prejudices were deep-seated; in the South, where I had not set foot since I left America twenty-five years ago; in that very South where, judging by what I had just been through, colored people must have been terribly unhappy.

I planned my journey carefully: I had become a reporter.

The colored university in Nashville—the capital of Tennessee, a southern state—had invited me to come and give a lecture to the students. At the same time, I had a great desire to go to St. Louis to visit my mother, whom I had not seen for years.

Here is where I would be reporting from.

To do this, I could not be Josephine Baker, music hall star—and a Frenchwoman, besides. I had to be a simple colored American, an ordinary Miss Brown. So I decided that I would be "Miss Brown." My chosen name seemed quite amusing, given the circumstances.

My plan was simple: to travel toward the South while doing everything that was forbidden for a "colored woman."

Jo wanted to join me.

"Absolutely not . . . I don't want to be with a white man. You can stay in New York. Besides, you've got to be there so someone can come and help me if they put me in prison."

"What if you get hurt—what if you get lynched?"

Jo is pessimistic sometimes. Not me.

Jo did insist, however, that I be accompanied by a friend of ours: a colored journalist, Jeff Smith.

I asked Jeff to let me do whatever I wanted. He was to be an impartial witness, never to intervene. He was also responsible for telling Jo if anything "really bad" happened to me: Jeff did not hide the fact that things could very well get out of hand for poor little Miss Brown upon her arriving in the South. That decided me for sure. Our departure was set for the day after next, but new adventures lay in store for us even before we left.

Jeff and I held a little council of war. I first wanted to be fully aware of the issue.

"You see," said Jeff, "there's actually a dividing line between the North and the South of the United States, a line called the Mason-Dixon Line, named after the two famous generals, one a Unionist, one a Confederate, who waged a fierce war against each other.[16] *In the journey we're going to make, this line passes through Washington, D.C. To its north is a liberal country where people more or less respect the law that grants full equality to colored people, although we've seen that's not always the case. To its south, the deeper you go, the more the old anti-colored mindset persists. For the people of the South, while American colored people aren't slaves anymore—though some people regard them as such—still they must not mix with white people."*

"Why do you say 'American colored people'?" I asked Jeff.

234

"I should have said 'colored Americans'; that's more accurate: because Confederates are specifically protecting themselves against those among their fellow countrymen who are colored."

"So, it's not only about skin color?"

"No, it's more complicated. For example, a French colored person is French; an Indian or a Chinaman is a free citizen, but a colored American is a 'black,' a 'Negro'—or worse, a 'nigger.'"

"But I know American colored people who are doing well," I said.

"Not in the South."

"Canada Lee is going to perform in the South . . . And Duke Ellington, and Lena Horne."

Jeff smiled sadly. "You haven't quite understood, Miss Baker—excuse me, Miss Brown . . . Canada Lee, Duke Ellington: When they go to the South they're a huge success. The whites celebrate them, they're proud of them."

"So?"

"Oh, it's simple! They're celebrated because they only perform with colored people. Try to get them onstage with some whites, and the theater will be set on fire."

"But Lena Horne is in films with white actors . . ."

"Yes, but they never give her a leading role. They just make her sing one or two songs, they cut down the sequences she appears in, and they remove her name from the publicity and the credits. Anyway, if you want to start your report, come with your husband and me to reserve our places on the sleepers."

At the first travel agency: "Two sleepers for Nashville, please."

The employee looked up at Jo, then Jeff. "Is it for you two?"

"Yes."

"Very sorry, there's no space left . . ."

It was the same farce in three other travel agencies.

"If we get sleepers," Jeff explained, "there's a chance they'll leave us in peace as far as Nashville. But if we have ordinary seats, they'll make us move into the special car for colored people. They attach one to every train when it crosses the famous Mason-Dixon Line."

On the one hand, we needed cabins; on the other, nobody wanted to give them to us . . .

"What if I went alone to reserve two berths?" Jo suggested.

"You could . . . But nothing says they'd let us keep them after the line, and it would make the report less accurate. What do you think, Miss Brown?"

Miss Brown (I really had become Miss Brown) was thinking that things were already getting complicated.

"Come with me to the newspaper office and we'll carry on with the experiment," Jeff said.

At the office, he picked up the phone and asked a fifth travel agency. "I would like two sleepers for Nashville."

"Certainly, sir!"

"Set them aside; I'm going to send my driver to pick them up."

"Okay!"

"Another thing: I'm a New Yorker, and my driver is a colored man. The second seat is for him. He's a nice boy; do you think he could keep his seat even in the South?"

The employee went quiet for a moment on the other end of the line. Then he said: "I do think that would be impossible."

Jeff insisted: "We fought in the war together. I would hate to cause him any offense."

The faraway voice became firmer: "I completely agree with you. I think it's stupid, but with those southerners . . . Okay, send him, I'll give him the two berths, and you can try and sort things out with the conductor when you get to the line."

One hour later, Jeff came back with our two tickets for the sleepers. The next day, at nine in the evening, we were on the train.

The beginning of the journey was uneventful: we were in the North. The next day, at lunchtime, we made our way to the dining car. Another colored passenger was with us—it was her first time on the famous Southern Railway.

"Excuse me, ma'am," she said to me. "Do we not need to dine behind a curtain?"

"Come with us," I replied, "and we'll find out."

Afraid of embarrassing herself, the poor woman lost her nerve upon reaching the dining car and made her escape. As for us, we were shown to a table and served a satisfying meal. However, before we had finished, the maître d' approached us and said: "I ask that you kindly hurry. You'll have just enough time to finish . . . We're getting close!"

We were indeed getting close—to the "line," that invisible yet terribly present line. It seems pointless to add that we had managed to finish our meal in peace, but just as we rose from the table to return to our compartment, four petty officers—four sergeants—entered, three white and one colored.

The maître d' hurried toward them. "I'm terribly sorry, but I can't serve you."

One of the white sergeants was far from amused. "And why's that? If the four of us just survived a good beating together, then the four of us can surely eat together!"

The maître d' was visibly uncomfortable. "Well, yes, if you had come earlier . . . *But now it's too late. We're just about to add a special car. If you would like to stay together, come this way . . ."*

He lifted the curtain for a moment, that famous curtain that had so frightened our fellow passenger earlier. Behind it were the tables for the colored passengers.

We were on the way back to our compartment, Jeff Smith and I, when the Southern Railway train stopped at a small station. It seemed just like the other small stations, so I paid no attention, not even to its name. I regret that now, because that was where an extra car was added to our train, complete with a sign that said, "COLORED."

All the colored passengers who had been mixed in with the white passengers since New York had to go and sit in this specially labeled car. We, and the woman who had been afraid to go for lunch, were left alone as far as Nashville, since we had booked luxury seats up to that point. And in America, a contract is a contract.

When I noticed that we had crossed the famous, the imperious, Mason-Dixon Line, I wanted to mark the occasion of officially arriving in the South by breathing in the new air. We had a one-hour stop.

"Stay on the train," I told Jeff Smith. "I'm going for a walk."

"All right, but don't do anything stupid . . . I'd rather have you back before we leave than have to fetch you from the town jail."

I had no intention of doing anything stupid. Moreover, since I was unaware of the things that were or were not permitted for a colored American, such as I was supposed to be, I was risking nothing by promising to be sensible.

And so, I jumped down onto the platform. Immediately, I saw that everything had changed. For the first time since my journey began, the *difference between people according to the color of their skin was crystal clear. The law of the South was asserted everywhere.*

Two signs: "WHITE" and "COLORED."

That was all. And it was more than enough to make one feel "not like the others," to realize that there was no use in even saying to oneself, "They may not want me, but I am within my legal rights." Those two signs confirmed that the only rights you had were the ones they gave you—excluding, above all, the right to mix with whites. There were two waiting rooms, two station cafés, two bathrooms, and everywhere: "WHITE . . . COLORED" . . . "WHITE . . . COLORED." No mixing, the golden rule.

We would see about that!

I entered the café that said "Whites" on the door. What would they do to me? All the tables were full; I walked through, not too confidently but not too awkwardly. I walked past the tables as if I was doing something entirely natural. I sensed heads raising, conversations coming to a halt. I kept moving. All eyes were turned toward me. I reached the counter, behind which were two busy waitresses.

"Two sandwiches and a kilo of apples, please."

The waitresses looked at me. I did not flinch. I think I even smiled. Then, very quickly as if wanting to get rid of me, one of the two girls handed me my sandwiches and apples, took my money, and . . . I left just as I had entered.

However, as I neared the door, I heard one of the customers say: "Quite a stranger here!"—as if looking for an excuse for not having intervened!

Once I had left the white café, I went into the colored café. There, I was struck by the customers' attitude—all colored, naturally. I thought I would at least come across an approving smile or a knowing look among all those colored people. But no, not at all! All I had before me were sullen, disapproving faces; some even appalled. I could not understand it. Even so, proud of myself, I returned to meet Jeff in our compartment. In the café, only a single pair of friendly eyes had met mine: those of a poor, dirty, mangy dog.

The train set off again. I asked Jeff to explain why those people in the colored café had acted so strangely.

"You scared them, Miss Brown."

"Scared them! Because I bought apples from that café for whites? Because they served me, and nothing happened?"

"Something could have happened. One of the customers could have provoked an incident . . . and when there's an incident between white and colored people, you never know how it will end."

I thought my experiment had been successful and that Jeff was exaggerating just as everyone else must have been. I told him so.

"You think I'm exaggerating? Well, read what's in this paper! It's all verifiable and verified."

He handed me the latest issue of a monthly magazine called Race Relations.

There, in the middle of the page:

BLOODSHED

. . . In Louisville, Kentucky, policeman John R. Womack, accompanied by another police officer, entered a bar where George Edward Kelly, a colored man, was having a drink. They accused him of causing public disorder and beat him to the ground. Since Kelly appeared to resist, they riddled him with bullets right in front of his father and brother.

The local police chief defended his subordinates and no charges were brought against them.

. . . In Rochester, New York, former G.I. Roland Price, a colored man, called the police because his tenant had not paid the rent. Policeman William Hammil arrived on the scene, accompanied by other policemen. Hammil took the tenant's side, angering Price, who moved his hand toward his pocket. He was immediately killed in a full-blown shootout. No weapons were found on his person. Coroner David H. A. Twater certified that Price's death had been caused by bullet wounds from shots fired by the officers, who were acting in the line of duty.

. . . In St. Louis, Missouri, Henry Blak, a Negro, was arrested by policeman Henry Reed on suspicion of stealing a blanket. As Blak tried to escape, Reed shot him in the head. The jury's verdict: "legal homicide."

I looked at Jeff Smith. He spoke to me softly:

"Now do you understand why they were scared in the café? But do keep reading, Miss Brown, and you'll see that there are, fortunately, other stories where even in the South, whites are rebelling against these abuses, these horrors. You'll see that white Americans are fighting this terrible injustice."

The train was still traveling toward Nashville.

"Keep reading Race Relations, *Miss Brown. You really will find some heartwarming pieces in there."*

I had closed the magazine. Jeff took it from where it rested on my knees, quickly leafed through it and handed it back to me, open.

"Read this!"

And so I did:

Jurors with Northern sympathies continue to put their racial passions before their duty and to work against all official decisions, leading to injustice of the worst kind. It was thus that the chief warden and four other wardens from Aiguila Prison, accused of having violated the civil rights of eight Negro prisoners, were acquitted after thirty minutes of deliberation.

I looked at Jeff Smith.

"The other side of the story comes straight after," he said.

Indeed, this Negro magazine did offer a little information that was somewhat encouraging, showing colored folk that despite everything, some white Americans were reflecting on how to improve their condition and finally give them the equality that was issued to them by the North, guaranteed them by law, but refused them by the South.

First, an official note:

In its report, the President's Committee on Civil Rights acknowledged the appalling violence committed by the police against minorities, and demanded that Congress establish a statute designed to prevent police brutality and the crimes that stem from it.

Another official note:

Montgomery, Alabama: It has been announced that Governor James E. Folsom has given the order to put an end to beatings and other forms of corporal punishment in all penitentiary establishments in Alabama. Instructions to this effect were given to State Prison Director Frank Boswell, leading to state-wide uproar and mass floggings of colored prisoners, both men and women.

We arrived in Nashville toward the end of the afternoon, where, for three days, Miss Brown became Josephine Baker again, invited by Charles S. Johnson, university president—this was a colored university where all the students are colored as well as the professors (except a few foreign ones).

I received a warm welcome. I gave several lectures, surrounded by three or four hundred students each time, boys and girls. The general theme was this: "France, North Africa, and racial equality in France." I would be standing; the audience would sit around me. As soon as I had finished my little talk, questions were fired at me from all directions.

"Are you an exception in France? Or else, can any colored man obtain first-rate employment? Give us details about how colored people are treated in France . . . In your country, would a white man let himself be treated by a colored doctor? Are there marriages between whites and colored people?"

I was dealing with an elite who were fighting for racial equality. And they could hardly believe the answers I had to their questions!

On the second evening I was introduced to a young girl who had finished her studies at the University of Nashville and who wanted to continue her education in a postgraduate school. However, there was no colored postgraduate school. Therefore, she had asked to be admitted into a white school. She was refused. The girl sent a letter to President Truman, who referred the matter to Congress. Congress voted, and it was decided that a colored university for postgraduate education would be created. In the meantime, she had been allowed to register at a white postgraduate school.

I watched her leave, without concern for the setbacks that awaited her, simply happy to be able to continue her education and proud to be the first female colored student to be able to do so.

Naturally, all our conversations revolved around the Negro question.

"Did you know," Dr. Johnson told me, "that every year in the United States, more than twelve thousand children with colored blood are born white, through mixed marriages? Despite the color of their skin, however, the Confederates still consider these 'white Negroes' to be colored. With a few rare exceptions, they move to a new town, and in their new place of residence, where nobody knows they have colored blood in their veins, they become whites, authentic whites. Unfortunately, these white Negroes are terrible toward the colored Negroes. Explain that as repression or using whatever psychological complex you like, that's how it is."

Dr. Johnson also told me:

"In our universities we train lawyers, doctors and engineers, but once they've obtained their degree, they have the greatest difficulty making use of it because it's assumed that they can only defend, treat or manage Negroes. That's why, on the trains, you see Negro employees and luggage porters who have been through university but who can't find any other job. Sometimes it leads to quite unexpected results . . . For example, tomorrow you're going to St. Louis, you'll be in the West; Confederate attitudes are more relaxed there. Imagine: in St. Louis, there was a mixed hospital where whites and Negroes were treated together. Now, the Negroes, through sheer tenacity, had a model hospital made, only for colored people . . ."

"What!" I exclaimed. "Here is a city where colored people are

treated as equal to white people and they're *the ones who refuse, who separate themselves?"*

Dr. *Johnson smiled. "There's a reason: Negroes have opened a hospital where they are treated by colored doctors and surgeons—treated and cured. So on the one hand, it's a way to give jobs to some of our own doctors; on the other hand, we're proving to white people that a Negro doctor or surgeon is just as capable as a white one."*

He went quiet, then continued. "It's something we're also proving to Negro patients because they often have an unfortunate inferiority complex—quite understandable, sadly! Generally, they'd trust a talentless white over a Negro genius."

St. Louis used to be where colored people would escape to. That is still the case today. My stepbrother was waiting for me at the station. To "please me," he had tipped off some journalists and photographers. They were searching the streets for children suffering from polio. One news photographer put a baby in my arms, a white baby, for a propaganda shot . . . And I considered the difference in morals between two regions only separated by a few hundred kilometers. That propaganda shot would have amounted to a crime in the South.

The reunion with my family—my mother, my brother, my sister, and my stepbrother—was a joy, as you may imagine.

My brother told me about one of the most important aspects of the Negro question. "There is a major controversy going on in the Senate: will the new United States Army include mixed regiments—white and colored people together—or units for white soldiers, and others for colored soldiers? Naturally, the Confederate senators—with Richard Russell at the top, a Georgian Democrat—are in favor of separation, or 'segregation.' Up until now, the army commission has rejected any amendments in this direction, because the majority are in favor of racial equality in the army. But the Confederate senators don't consider themselves defeated. They've decided to use whatever means necessary to make sure their point of view prevails. But they'll have to make concessions. They're already accepting that there could be mixed units, but they ask that all white people who request it are not included in them. Mixed units are a huge step forward, considering that the last war's military regime had no such thing. But as soon as President Truman made it known that he was determined to do everything possible to completely eradicate the army's racial separation regime, Russell went on the offensive. He declared that he would 'filibuster'—that is, since the rules allow it, he'll read the Bible for hours, for days on end, until the majority are fed up and give in. And so the Negro question risks delaying the entire military reorganization of the United States."

After spending a few days with my family in St. Louis, I returned to New York, where, alerted by telegram, my husband was waiting for me at the station. "Miss Brown" had disappeared. Josephine was regaining contact with the enormous American city, staying in a comfortable hotel whose owner had formally declared that he did not intend to realize, as soon as she arrived, that his apartment was in fact reserved for somebody else.

I caught up on some offers I had received during my absence. Among other things, I was being offered the starring role in a show to mark the reopening of Café Society, the biggest and most elegant cabaret in New York. I also had a copious number of letters. One letter in particular struck me—one that appeared to be a sort of conclusion to what I was already indulgently calling my report. But first I must explain that the United States does not have a national theater, nothing that even remotely resembles an institution like the Comédie Française, which enjoys enormous prestige abroad.

In 1935, Congress had in fact passed a law establishing the American National Theater and Academy (which the craze for acronyms had immediately renamed ANTA). However, until now, this national theater did not really exist. At the end of the war, a committee decided to move ANTA out of the theoretical realm and actually create a theatrical institution whose objective—far from making a profit—would be to bring the classic masterpieces to the whole of the United States, with performances by the biggest stars, as well as giving young, talented writers and actors their big break.

In particular, this letter asked me—me, a colored artist—to give my first performance in New York in aid of ANTA. Needless to say, I was very touched, especially after everything I had put up with during my journey. Needless to say, too, that I happily accepted.

Just as, until now, there had not been a national theater institution in America, until recent years there were no purely American operatic works.

The first composer to write an American opera was George Gershwin, around fifteen years ago. He had Porgy and Bess performed on Broadway, where the rehearsals were completely shrouded in mystery. Gershwin's reputation was such that all the seats were reserved in advance for the first twenty performances.

But on preview night, the spectators crammed into the theater were frozen with astonishment. For the first time on Broadway, colored *actors were performing with white actors. There was outrage. However, Gershwin's work was so powerful, so beautiful—and the first American opera—that it carried the day. It was a triumph. It played for two years running. Since then, no one had dared to repeat Gershwin's experiment. At least not until 1947, when some daring directors put on an operetta at the Forty-sixth Street Theatre, this one also performed by white and colored people, which proves first and foremost that there are still white American actors who do not consider it disgraceful to perform with colored actors.*

During my stay in New York, this operetta, Finian's Rainbow, *was one of the biggest successes of the season. I spoke to Lee Sabinson and William Katzell, the show's producers:*

"We're so happy," they told me, "that we've decided to shoot a film version of Finian's Rainbow.*"*

As I congratulated them, they added, a little sadly:

"Our play ran for eighteen months. So the film will also be a sure success. And despite that, well, no Hollywood producer wants to risk shooting a mixed-cast film. Since we're stubborn, we've decided to go and make Finian's Rainbow *in a studio in Mexico. Mind you, we have no idea whether a cinema chain will accept our film once it's finished. We'll give it a shot anyway, in the hope that by that time, maybe, racial prejudices will have decreased enough for a cinema audience to accept our film as enthusiastically as theater audiences did our play."*

No Jews, no dogs, no niggers . . .

Can you blame me for being obsessed with this phrase, these ferocious words that I heard people say even in New York itself, and by good people? Are we just bugs to these good Americans? Did we walk on water to come to their country? Is it honorable in today's world, tell me, that in America—in these American cities that pride themselves on being at the forefront of all progress— that after a certain time in the evening, Jews and Negroes can't leave their houses, that they're banished as if they were plague-ridden, or face consequences that are pretty much covered by laws that are shameful in themselves?

What a despicable farce!

More despicable, of course: conflict between brothers of the same race. There are, in the United States, thirteen million Negroes; every year, twelve thousand white Negroes are born among them. These white Negroes, with their blue eyes, are the others' worst enemies, merciless traitors, crueler to their own kind than white extremists and, even more than their own kind, at the mercy of the situations handed down to them, the business deals, the schemes, the money, and the lowest kind of conformism.

More astounding, more revolting, even more monstrous still is the drama that plays out between two races that are each equally cursed.

I'm on the "niggers'" side. I feel no glory or humiliation about that. I made no choice.

On the other hand, I love dogs. I love all animals. I've noticed too often how much men and women who don't like them can lose their sense of humanity, all their empathy, even the meaning of life itself.

You've really got to have courage to speak out about things, in the hope that people—who, you pray from the bottom of your heart, will never be victims again—will open their eyes, open them first to themselves, and understand, improve themselves, finally change things. These things must change. They must.

I would have never believed that Jews, who are subject everywhere to bigotry, tragedy, and resentment, would be capable of behaving as badly as they do in America toward colored people.

I'm not unreliable, am I? I don't think I'll be accused of lying. I'd have too much trouble in the future. I was married to a Jew. I hold nothing against him. His mother will always have a big place in my heart. I was a part of his family, of other Jewish families, too, where I found people whom I love, whom I admire, whom I'd defend if someone attacked them. But the terrifying exploitation of colored people by Jews in America: no, truly, it can't be ignored. We can't stay silent. That's not possible.

When one thinks about the massacre of Jews in Europe, in Africa, in Asia, and of the fact that there are Jewish refugees from all over the world in New York, that there always have been, many of whom don't speak English, don't want to, and will never speak English. When one hears that in the entire world, it's Jews who shout and beg for mercy the loudest—and they have good reason for that—to demand justice and equality between people, and then you see how they treat colored people in America; in fact, how can we not manage to persuade ourselves that what they're doing is emotional fraud, that they're only demanding equality for themselves, only the rights that let them be as evil, as vicious, as their enemies?

It was for them, was it not, that we went to war, because the Germans were condemning Jews and colored people—how can they justify behaving worse than the white Americans toward those poor Harlemites and the rest?

In Africa, I sang in camps for Jewish soldiers, colored soldiers, and Greeks, Poles, Belgians . . .

And now?

Oh! Amid the pain of these things, how I've missed the war. There was a purity to all the soldiers, a little brotherliness. When there was bread, it was shared; when there was nothing to eat, they'd console each other, without worrying about skin color or the beliefs in people's heads.

In Harlem, some Jews are reducing colored people to slaves. In Harlem, all the landlords are Jews. They exploit all the colored people. All the cinemas, all the five-and-dimes in Harlem, belong to Jews. The shop assistants are colored, and they're swindled like nowhere else. Colored people can't work without Jews. They can't go and work on Broadway without going through Jews. They depend completely on Jews. They're in the palm of their hand, subject to their demands.

And not one colored person raises their voice, not one would dare, against the Jews. Colored people know, to their cost, that they could die of hunger if they protest the treatment they suffer from Jews.

"I'll give you the opportunity of a lifetime," the Jews say to the colored people in Harlem, whatever profession the colored people may choose. And the colored people are forced to accept the opportunity the Jews offer them because, otherwise, they'd have no chance at life no matter what they did. An opportunity from the Jews is bondage for colored people. When a colored artist, for example, earns good pay—three thousand dollars a week is the most—the Jew in charge of salaries takes an unbelievable percentage from each one, everywhere, every time.

Every colored boxer's manager is a Jew. There are countless colored boxers who only get one tenth of what their broken noses earn them. Many of the gangsters are Jews. They're less dangerous than other Jews for the colored people of Harlem and elsewhere.

The Jews are moving further and further out of Harlem.

They're pushing the "blue bloods" out of Park Avenue, out of Riverside Drive, where until not long ago, they weren't accepted any more than colored people. They're making the old Rockefellers move away, families with old money, all those who made good on their ventures. The Jews have money, too, lots, always more money. And they pay in cash. They've found the trick to secretly buying what they were banned from, all these tricks under false names.

They're buying more and more apartment blocks in the best areas of New York, and all the staff who keep them running—whom they treat how they want, pay what they want—are colored.

Do the Jews not realize what they're doing? Why are they doing this? Have they really come from all over the world to do this? Can we believe they're sincere when they complain about and blame other people? Don't they see they're summoning yet more tragedy onto themselves, onto their children, too, that when the time comes, they'll be more blamed than pitied?

Believe me, I had to check before accepting all this. I found it so difficult to believe it could be true . . . I thought about those Jews I'd only recently admired in Jerusalem. Those ones, around the Great Synagogue, were so handsome, with their big hats decorated with animal tails. They walked majestically. They leaned on long canes. They were like serene, benevolent prophets, with long sideburns reaching to their chests. They wore the nobility of their poverty without pride. I liked them more than the priests—Catholic, Protestant, or Orthodox—who wouldn't stop arguing outside the church doors around the city.

Yes, I thought about them in the streets of Harlem.

And I saw the Wailing Wall again, smooth, polished, worn by hands, foreheads, lips. Also in my memory, Tel Aviv: a unique achievement in the world, rising up from dry rocks, a beautiful, brand-new city that makes you trust those who built it, when you walk its streets.

Oh! Why, in an ironic twist of fate for both of them, must the poor colored people of Harlem be a punching bag for the Jews, who've forgotten their forefathers' story?

And the poor colored people in America, in New York, in Harlem, those with no money, who are exploited and oppressed, where do they go to find support, consolation, distractions? To someone else who takes advantage of their misery and their naïveté—a colored man who's had an unbelievable influence on them—to Father Divine.

Oh! Father Divine . . .

It's only in America that one can admire a Buddha from the underbelly like him. Not Buddha, I meant boudin—black pudding. He's round and greasy like a black pudding. I watched him going about his work, but he would not meet me in private. He'd caught on that I wasn't on his side. No, really; his business is unacceptable.

Father Divine earns millions, pays no taxes, runs circles around the police and policemen, and takes advantage of simple souls. He has ruthless power. Don't go telling his followers that their living God is nothing but a crook. They're so devoted they'd murder you. You'd be lynched if you challenged the great Holy Father Black Pudding.

Father Divine has miraculous skill. His church is in fact just an enormous restaurant, where people are served cheap, generous meals of all kinds, with white bread, cakes, specialities my race enjoy.

There are masses of people, naturally, mostly women, and quite a few white ones among them, by the way. It's uncanny, disturbing, the lunches, the teas, the dinners, at Father Divine's. The way the women glorify him borders on hysteria. It builds, it builds, as everyone eats, prays, and shouts.

The servers are angels, dressed as angels. They're all named after flowers: Angel Violet, Angel Tulip, Angel Rose, Angel Begonia, Angel Daisy, Angel Carnation, Angel Lily . . .

There's a microphone in the middle of the big room. A voice rumbles through it, coming from a set of bedrooms, small halls, and lounges above the restaurant.

The voice calls: "Angel Rose? Angel Daisy?"

Father Divine's secretary is a white girl with a refined white voice.

"Angel Forget-Me-Not . . . Angel Mignonette . . . Angel Clematis!" The Holy Father is summoning those who wanted to speak to him.

Everyone looks at these people with admiration. It's an honor to be called like this. People pay for it in many different ways. And all of a sudden, a woman stands up. She's euphoric; she thanks the microphone god and starts to shout.

"You rightly said, Father, that we would have snow. The sun was shining like it was the middle of summer, like the month of July, but then the sky suddenly went dark and snow started falling!"

Another woman: "I had a broken leg. He said one word, and I felt absolutely fine!"

And another . . . And another . . . All of them, eventually, men and women. And Father Divine listens to all of this from the depths of his sanctuary, where the smell from the kitchens also reaches. And between the kitchens and the sanctuary's secret location, millions of greenbacks stop by.

Father Divine lives in New Jersey, half an hour away from New York, to avoid the taxes. He lives between jurisdictions. He has to leave New York every evening before sundown. An armored car—he has several—waits for him at the door of his church restaurant.

Father Divine returns to Mrs. Divine, who is white. The Negro god has a white wife.

I went to eat at Father Divine's.

The angel who came to serve me put a beautiful linen napkin on my plate. Oh no, my dear angel, no . . . There's been a mistake. I didn't want it. Give me a little paper napkin like everyone else. The angel reported back to the good Lord, and apparently, it made a very bad impression. One does not refuse Father's graces. Any discussion became impossible. Oh well.

I don't mean to go on, but it really is exploitation, and it isn't the hot meals, the white bread, and the cakes, but emotions, emotional fraud. That, you know, is what's infinitely pitiable. I don't like it when love is manipulated like that. But there are so many others; men try it all the time. They talk about love. They really like it, all of them, when you speak to them about love, in one way or another . . . love or brotherhood. When you happen to look a little closer, with any of them at all, is there anything beneath their words?

Life gave me three Mamas who share my heart: Mama from St. Louis, Mama Lion, and Mama Bouillon. I also have Pepito's family, and I have a husband whom I love because he's good and really understands that life isn't an operetta.

After the America trip, before the Folies Bergère rehearsals, I was in Italy with Jo, in Rome. The Pope gave us a private audience. I simply told him as many things as I could about my experience with different people and countries.

10

A FINAL WORD ON
THE CELEBRITIES OF THE TIME

've seen lots of famous people, but few impressive ones. Everyone does what they can. I most admire those who work the most. Especially those who find joy in their work.

I'm not intimidated by anyone. Everyone is made with two arms, two legs, a belly, and a head. It's enough to think about that, to look, in order to notice a great quality or a small flaw. In any case, I don't judge. I don't want to judge. We all have enough troubles, deep down.

My colleagues on the stage are all very good, but I'm not interested in that anymore. On the other hand, I want to understand.

The ones who stay young for a long, long time are the strongest. Stay young, lively, fearless, free—and go fast—that's what they teach you in America. The pity is you get used to money later on.

I'd like never to get old, to march to a drum, the drum of youth—but without strict orders—my own drum. Dance, sing, be free. Maybe it will kill me. Doesn't matter if sometimes your skin and your lungs rip, so what . . .

They did me the honor of thinking I was a fool. I still have respect. I don't have it in me to be a snob. I don't like snobby people, snobby animals. People have told disgusting stories about me. I've no need for them. And neither do I have any explanation to give. God doesn't leave me. He's here, inside me; he is my strength and my freedom. I use all my time to live.

But I can give you a few portraits or, rather, a few outlines. A mark out of ten, simply. Because I'm cautious, you know . . . Despite myself.

Diplomacy, always diplomacy, tact, expectations, poise. Oh, là là! If I said straight—or let us say—even 1 percent of what I think, what I've seen, really seen, what I know . . . Poor Josephine! It would be over. One day, like in the fairy tales, we'll write the truth, the whole truth, if you still want us to. It'll do us good; others, too. There aren't many of them, sadly, lovers of the truth! Until then, we must all work. Live. That's the most important thing. And remember, Monsieur Sauvage, that all people ask is to be flattered. For the most part, all that keeps a good relationship going is flattery, nothing more. So, switch on the charm, please.

Let's only talk about people dear to our hearts.

Monsieur Vincent Auriol came to see the books on sale at the Colonial Exhibition, where I was at a stand one afternoon in '48. He stopped, said hello. "Bonjour, Monsieur le Président." And he talked. He also has a bit of an accent that lilts through his smile. A touch of fatherly kindness, straightforward, as required. I like that. In my opinion, he's the most likable French citizen—that's his job. Monsieur Vincent Auriol, a citizen president, chubby.

King Gustaf of Sweden. The modest king. He welcomed me to his home, with his family, several times. I saw him again in France, when he was traveling through Paris to go and play tennis in the south. He'd be a king in name only were he without his special grace—*barakah,* as the Moroccans say—and his radiant kindness. People really are scared that he'll shatter. They're scared out of friendship. Because he's one of those people whom you admire more the less they take the spotlight, even though he towers above other people like a maypole. And the people love him. Why? Because here's an old monarch who's keeping safe the youngest, liveliest nation there is and, up until now—it's as clear as day—a country that's healthy. May this country keep its king and its health for a long time.

She stands quite apart from Negro art, does Katherine Dunham. I've seen her shows. I went back three times. I received her—with such joy, as you can imagine—the tall, thin, the elegant Katherine Dunham, intelligent right down to her fingertips. She has the fingers of a learned woman and enamel eyes like an Egyptian statue. I introduced her on French radio. I'm passionate about everything that can testify for our race.

Imagine that Katherine's dance partners were dressed differently, that they weren't colored: they'd be like the Ballets Russes, the same caliber. Negro art that's more than stylized—it's outclassed. Nothing wild or primitive left, in the general sense of the words. Look what we're capable of.

It's important, and I hope they're always crowned with success, efforts like these—I do as best I can—for the benefit of colored people, the idea we have of them that's so out of date. Katherine Dunham is already our great Katherine.

He's so funny—this general who doesn't joke around—a strict general. A sweet army man, that's what he looks like. Well dressed; neat, like a drawing for a Philadelphia catalog. Righteous, tall, refined. A model of military elegance, kind and thoughtful, but uncompromising. He doesn't obey: General Clark commands.

Luigi Pirandello, I used to call him my uncle. He'd always sit in a box at the Casino, very close. He'd come to mine at Le Vésinet, in those days. He liked it there.

My Uncle Pirandello was a little bearded man, white. His pointy goatee was always moving. He was anxious—in fact, he rather acted like a headstrong nanny goat, with his sparkling eyes. He used to dream about writing a play for me, and he did write part of one. He'd jump from one topic to the next. He'd laugh like the baby goats in Sicily when they've found a little bit of green grass; then he was no longer anxious, but sweet.

Ah, Colette! Of course . . . I found myself a sister, I mean a real soulmate, with her love for animals, cats, dogs, plants, too, and flowers.

She writes to me on lacy paper. She says I have a soul that inspires her to write to me on lacy paper, white paper, pink paper, sometimes blue or cream, and Japanese paper. Colette's letters, I keep them like talismans.

There's a tone in her voice that makes her sound more like real life. It makes you sound more real, an accent, wouldn't you say? It connects you. You can't float away.

And what eyes! Dark portals. They'd make any woman beautiful. They caress everything they look at.

And on top of that, her hair! She's so lucky. What hair—not like mine—it's bubbly, it's smoky, her hair. It evaporates. Mine sticks to me.

Colette, I love her! She's very familiar with the music hall. And she's generous. And yet she's been backstage everywhere.

I met the princess and Peter of Greece in Beirut. We have stayed friends. Very dear ones, because they are beautiful above all. And royals from within. Not at all out of pretentiousness or an official gesture, oh no! They're *elegantly* intelligent. That's rare, don't you think? And there isn't one art form out of them all that doesn't interest them. They listen and they watch with elegance. They want to share. That's what makes them even more wonderful than I can express, you see.

Look what he wrote for me, Maurice Dekobra, on one of his books: "To Josephine Baker, to my fairy of the tropics, to the unforgettable creator of the Siren, in memory of the Parisian jungle. With very best wishes."

Maurice Dekobra is a man of the jungle. He thinks it's a Parisian thing. Oh well. To tell the truth, we had our moments while filming. He had me rolling in flour. That cost us very dearly, but we can move past it. You say, Monsieur Sauvage, that you saw him on the beaches in the south of France, where he had his head screwed on right, dressed like a music hall cowboy with blue-, red-, and green-checked shirts and bandanas. I didn't. I'm astounded. He was always like everyone else, like an international gentleman here, very much the man at the bar, in his way, poker straight, even his face is all straight lines, bony, even, wouldn't you say, with ridges, but kind.

The Negus's son is my pal, certainly a good pal, but a spoiled child. He's like every other spoiled child.

Archie Roosevelt, another spoiled child, is the president's son. At home everywhere, and always in a good mood. A go-getter, intelligent, carefree. He drinks neat, and then his skin goes transparent like the outside of a red balloon. He's sensitive. You wouldn't go near him with a pin, but he's very kind.

How many adjectives have you got, Monsieur Sauvage? Well, you'll need them all—your very best—for His Highness Moulay Larbi el Alaoui, the first cousin of His Majesty the Sultan of Morocco, and for his stepbrother, His Excellence Mohamed Menebhi. I owe them a lot, all French people owe them a lot, the women in Morocco will owe them a lot, and one day all the Muslim women in Africa, too.

Moulay Larbi is a giant with a commanding presence, a heart to match, a spirit, too, and courtesy always on his lips. He knows everything. He's the most modern Moroccan. A statesman. Yes, I can judge, for I've seen lots of statesmen from up close. I never said much, but I sure was watching.

One of those who really impressed me in France, with their knowledge, their approachable manner, and their sincerity most of all— I mean a human sincerity, informal, direct, and open—is President Herriot. He's an expert at all those topics for argument or strong emotions that can come up unexpectedly. You'd imagine he'd just been thinking about them. And he has an ear for music, a nice laugh, too, such a big, friendly laugh.

Yes, the most persuasive politicians for me are the men whose experience doesn't browbeat you but, rather, charms you; who keep their most confident and most cheerful manners conserved like a weapon. Another example: President Monnerville.

. . . But we were in Africa.

Mohamed Menebhi, who was awarded the Legion of Honor in 1949, really deserved not one but two. My dear Marrakshi friend is more solid, he's chubbier, than Moulay Larbi, with eyes that burn like black fire and a little mustache. In Morocco, the men really know how to wear a mustache.

Mohamed Menebhi and Moulay Larbi decided to work to ensure that the women in Morocco would have nothing left to envy the Egyptian and Turkish women for. It's still not easy, but they'll get there. They deserve our praise.

Monsieur Georges Duhamel was in Buenos Aires; so was I. We had lunch together. "Maestro, you have the voice of a turtledove!" Georges Duhamel strokes his hands and wraps you up without your feeling like you're being touched. Before you know it, he's charmed you. He crosses his fingers. He smiles through his glasses. He smooths everything out with the gentle way he talks, even when he's being critical, and his criticism goes even further. His gaze is always alert.

Monsieur Duhamel asked if he could come and see me. I said no. Not here. Later. I'm never happy with myself. I was even less so in Buenos Aires. I'll let you know.

He's still waiting. But I noticed how much he loves music. One evening in the French embassy in Buenos Aires, Jo and Gabriel Bouillon played Bach's *Double Violin Concerto* for him, with piano accompaniment. His eyes were closed. He was drinking in the music of the violins. He doesn't like all that American bopping around.

King Farouk, five, six times, here and there, in palaces, in public, in private, at the theater, when I was in the army. King Farouk's people love him. I felt it when I was traveling through Egypt.

When you're talking about a king, you must first try and find out what his people think of him. Nothing else is more important.

The Egyptian people also really love France. People speak French in Egypt. All the Egyptians you meet on your way through the cities have their French school diploma. Okay. Let's hope we don't forget.

The novelist Massimo Bontempelli wrote this for me: "*Con entusiasmo immenso dopo una indimenticabile serata di spettacolo di grande arte.*" "With immense enthusiasm after an unforgettable evening—a show of true art."

For Massimo, I'll say, in Italian, *ammirabile.* Italian is gentle on the tongue like Italy is gentle on the eyes. If France didn't exist, I would have chosen Italy to live and die in.

A review of Monsieur Francis Carco. *Lu, vu, entendu,* to quote that rather mild slang. All in all, not a bad man. He isn't obnoxious. He's a poet. He has a crafty smile, on the corner of a street in Paris, a voice like mine, songs neither low- nor high-pitched. He wrote in a book he gave me: "With my great admiration." He's nice. I don't think he looks like Napoleon.

Some people have fame but not talent. Others have talent but not yet the fame they deserve. Michel Gyarmathy, an artist, set designer, and director, always in search of something new, is one of the latter. I'm not saying this because he's at the Folies. No. Michel always seems to be apologizing for having so much talent. He's modest, he moves gently, this Hungarian in Paris, with little pale eyes that squint to see the lines, the colors. And he has thick crepe soles on his shoes so he doesn't make too much noise. But he works, he's worked so much in silence. He's quietly audacious, makes an effort to be kind. He dared to make me into Mary, Queen of Scots, and Joséphine de Beauharnais. He designed beautiful dreams for me around their characters. He achieved in the music hall what only seemed possible in a big, traditional theater. Don't you think he deserves to be famous? He could have killed me. Thanks to his magnificent costumes, I was reborn.

I don't like paintings that much, generally speaking—not modern paintings, anyway. I can't understand something that can so easily make me giggle without knowing why. I don't know much, it's true. But I've often spent hours wandering through museums or big exhibitions alone. I've happily got myself lost. Looking at paintings is an excuse to daydream. I don't get excited by what makes them famous. But I do prefer the Italian classics to the others. I'll never grow tired of Guardi's paintings.

I've had my portrait done a few times. You know that when I was starting out, I posed for the Beaux-Arts in Paris. That's how I met van Dongen, who became my friend, sometimes a casual one. But he's a free man. He may be modern, but he has a beard, and his paintings seem older to me than he looks, in a good way, don't you think?

Before the war, too, I posed for Jean-Gabriel Domergue. He was in fashion. He painted two portraits of me that he took to America; it was a revolution. A colored woman, imagine, among high-society women in the land of money . . . What sacrilege!

Monsieur Domergue came to see me in North Africa during the war, in Morocco, at a time when I was unwell. I'd lost twenty-five kilos. He was hopeless: "Oh, your beautiful buttocks!" he said. "Your beautiful buttocks have disappeared." This gracious society painter doesn't concern himself with high-society language.

Oh, Noël Coward! I adore his lovely face. He's a guy with a lovely face. A model Englishman. The hero of the English troops in Africa.

The most famous stars in London didn't really mind, you know, when they had to go and perform far away, on the edge of the battlefields.

Noël Coward, an author, actor, and presenter, lavished his time and all his talents on the English soldiers in the desert. I saw him in a tent in the middle of the camps with the great artist Vivien Leigh. He's funny, all flushed and bubbly, clever and sweet, all chubby. What a lovely face! His smile, he doesn't keep it to himself, he gives it to you, you can take it. Some men keep their smiles stashed away; his is a gift. You walk away with Noël Coward's smile.

Some claim I was received in Madrid by General Franco. Why say such things? Apparently we even discussed Spain's future. Oh, là là! I'd rather they had me playing the castanets in Montserrat. I didn't meet Franco; I met his brother, the ambassador to Lisbon. A diplomat with perfect manners. A model diplomat. *Play?* . . . *Ready.* Always dignified. He's an exception.

Finally, I like it when one has to lift one's head to look at a man, and I like men who tend to be quiet when they have something good and private to them on their mind, something pure in their eyes. I'm talking about feelings. I'm not bothered about politics. General de Gaulle is a great man.

He always seems a little sad, distant, like he's trying to stand back a little to judge something. Always seems like he's thinking about France as if *you* were France when he looks at you; even the least important people who approach him are deemed worthy of that look.

He doesn't want France to be walked all over, to be trampled on in any way. He said no to everybody on that point. I saw it for myself, in the secret role I had among his people.

He has principles. He's so honest, it compels loyalty. His children never gained anything from his status. He used to hide them. He urged them to do their duty without ever showing off.

During the war and the occupation in Africa—he did a lot for them, you know, French Africa—he only had one uniform, and that uniform was well worn. It was ironed quickly every time there was an official meeting.

At the theater in Algiers, for my first show in support of the Free French forces, he took the presidential box with Madame de Gaulle. His ordnance officer came looking for me. General de Gaulle introduced me to Madame de Gaulle, and he made me sit next to her, in his own seat. The general's seat, can you imagine!

And Madame de Gaulle, I can still see her. All she'd dream about was living quietly with her children in a little house. Oh!

These military men . . . I can see her very well, humble and modest, with her gray yarn stockings, her little flat-heeled shoes, with a little barrette. She'd so charmingly call me "dirty little Gaulliste."

Future, future . . .

Before a crowd of faces, like in the theater when you look through the little gap in the curtain.

The future . . .

Of course! I'll dance, sing, and perform all my life; that's what I was born for. To live is to dance; I'd like to die breathless, exhausted, at the end of a dance or a song—but not in the music hall.

I'm tired of this artificial life, fed up of being lashed by the spotlights. I haven't enjoyed the job of being a star. It disappoints me now. I'm disgusted by all the intrigue that surrounds a star. Everything a star must do, everything they must accept, promise, put up with constantly, this star, it disgusts me. Bad things, sad things. My soul is beaten down now. Enough.

The Americans had the idea of making a film about my life. And they asked Lena Horne to play the role of Josephine, no less . . . Americans are like that. But *I* will star in the film of my life. And I'll leave the stage for good. I'll go and settle down in the south of France. I'll live in Les Milandes. I'd like to live there in peace, with my husband, with our families, with my memories, among children and animals.

My last wish, Marcel, you who have been my poet—write this down—is to turn into a fairy; that's what I really want: to be the fairy godmother to a little French village, to have everyone around me, far away . . .

AFTERWORD

Jean-Claude Bouillon-Baker

2021 was a year that ended in triumph. Paris stood on the shoulders of human dignity, its sky alight with tolerance as the flags of fidelity and commitment were unfurled.

Not so long ago, any who witnessed this scene would have struggled to imagine the Bird of the Isles, the Belle Sauvage, the Black Venus, the "idol of irony and gold" making her entry into the Panthéon mausoleum in Paris. But on Tuesday, November 30, 2021, the French capital did not wish her "Farewell" as it had forty-six years earlier, in the guise of a state funeral on the steps of La Madeleine church. This time it was a "Hello!"—a welcome into her new immortality. This highest of national honors put her name on equal footing with that of the great French public figures. With her deep sense of humility, she would have rejected this crown as too heavy for a mere mortal to wear. And yet we are not dreaming. A former child from the street really does now share a vault with the great war writer Maurice Genevoix.

Since her funeral, a period that seems both long and short, she has occupied a growing place in the hearts of women and men. Two generations of curious minds have learned to understand her better and to appreciate the inspiring beauty of her extraordinary nature. Clear and direct, her journey has been revealed to them as an unambiguously straight line; neither hidden crossroads nor a single swerve into the ditches of easier choices have presented themselves along the way. The journey of one who accomplished before ever thinking of self-accomplishment.

Now, Josephine, you can nestle into the fraternal embrace of Aimé Césaire, bard of the negritude literary movement; of the mischievous Alexandre Dumas, his one-quarter black blood whitened by his descendants, who, if he had known you, would have recounted your saga splendidly; you can mix your blood with the heroic pulse of Toussaint Louverture, abolisher of slavery in his country, Haiti, which you sang about in your deeply moving tones . . . All four of you welcomed into the Panthéon after the thousand and one meanders of a slavery that singled out your skin and caused your spirits to revolt. You will rub shoulders with the great literary minds of Victor Hugo and Émile Zola, universal defenders of the poor and denigrators of injustice; you, whose time in classroom education was fleeting at best, you will stand beside them for your lifetime of wisdom and initiative. Marie Curie, Simone Veil, Geneviève de Gaulle-Anthonioz . . . These other admirable women have taken your hand and form your cortège. Voilà! Your destiny has been fulfilled, at the utmost boundary between the hearts of the living and the souls of the dead. Now you can let go and enter another eternity in the same way you moved through every stage of your life: with panache.

This book is a miracle. It allows us to "hear" Tumpy—the childhood nickname used by those closest to her throughout her life; Josie, the burgeoning teenager discussing her dead-end roles, performing in colored theaters only; Josephine, the iconoclastic performer established on both sides of the Atlantic; and Josephine Baker, the uncontested icon. The multitude of voices she harbored come joyfully alive: they marvel at the beauty of every single thing in every country discovered; they embrace her and retain her essence as she moves from one home to another; to later reconstruct her, piece by piece, in her dream home of Périgord stone. She worries about inequality; she is touched by humankind's many colors and the polyphony of audiences around the world. Her childhood and her magnificent teenage years are filled with animals big and small, without preference for species or beauty. This voice, rescued from the past and the sentiment of the times, gushes with crystal-clear kindness and spontaneous generosity: the sign of a heart fortified by poverty and injustice. But she also displays unfading devotion and commitment, to herself and to others, during dark and fateful times; she pulsates with optimism, faith, and resolution during the steel storm of war. After the war, her last marriage is completed by the gift of twelve little ones; indeed, when she passed away, it was as the mother she had become—the one gifted to me by Providence.

Under the ever tender, generous, and poetic pen of Marcel Sauvage, sometimes pared back to the merest sketch (and what a wonderful twist of fate to have met the Belle *Sauvage* de Paris), this book is a shining light from start to finish. Paris married her, and she married the whole of France. The wedding was triumphantly extravagant: it was the Roaring Twenties, an enchanted interlude before the advent of the Popular Front. She danced atop this whirlwind of pleasures, parties, and libertarian artistic performances. At the heart of this uninterrupted scintillation, she would be its Black star.

Then came the war. What path should she take? She was known to keep her word and possessed a taste for secrets, too . . . And so it was that she became an eager, trusted member of the French intelligence services: an inevitable step for the Frenchwoman she had become. She almost lost her life a thousand times, but like the phoenix she was, she soared toward her last triumph.

Those who gravitated around Josephine were infected with an unconditional affection for her; a magnetic force, a star, she was mystifying yet so real, familiar yet enigmatic. Even those most resistant to effusive outpourings succumbed to her effortless, natural charms right up until her last moments on earth. On the day when no one could really believe she was dead, an English historian left these few words in the book of condolences in Monaco: "She was adorable, mystical, magical, unpredictable, idealistic, mad, generous and warm . . ." Adorable for her extreme kindness, a Tanagra of mischief, a girl on wings . . . Mystical in her natural form, wild, every god in one . . . Magical whether dressed, undressed, onstage, onscreen, or in real life; a magician, for her gift of never aging . . . Unpredictable for the instinct worn like a necklace and the conviction running through her veins . . . An idealist, for the utopian fairies who blessed her at birth and for her inalienable dream of a potential fraternity. Mad, for she was human, too human. Generous in every respect . . . Generous to a fault. And warm, a river of love and tenderness for every living being on this earth.

A voluntary daughter of France, she expressed gratitude with body and soul for what became her true country, in a life that sang of devotion and commitment. She teaches us that we must love the ground we stand on and that we must love men and women, deeply, wherever they are in the world, for what they are: equal human beings. An exemplary figure of triple resilience—female, Black, and poor—she independently refutes all the fatalism that oppresses, confines, and imprisons willpower within old woes.

The Panthéon may have closed its doors on a radiant fighter who now luminesces like a beacon above us all—with others from the past and indeed the future. But this book opens another door: upon the unique voice that characterized one of the most extraordinary women of the twentieth century.

TRANSLATORS' ACKNOWLEDGMENTS

This translation was more than a collaboration between two translators. We have several people to thank. Thanks go to Anya Edmond-Pettitt from the Institute of Race Relations for helping with archival material and pointing us to the translator's note in *Resolutely Black: Conversations with Françoise Vergès,* translated by Matthew Smith; Mona Horncastle for her thorough knowledge of Josephine Baker in the context of Austria and Germany (Horncastle's biography of Baker is out now in German: *Josephine Baker: Weltstar—Freiheitskämpferin—Ikone*); Aglika Angelova for the Hamburg references; and Helen Vassallo of the University of Exeter for sources.

For specific terms, we would like to thank the Musée de la Résistance Nationale and the Musée de l'Ordre de la Libération; Yasmine Seale for the conversation about *One Thousand and One Nights;* Claire Savina and Leonie Rau for their input on transliteration from Arabic; Jennyfer Miara, Nadiyah Abdullatif, and Ferroudja Djaroun for their deciphering of period French; and Georgia Wall for the translation from Italian.

Last but certainly not least, we are indebted to Brent Hayes Edwards's *The Practice of Diaspora* for guiding our translation choices for racialized terms.

SONG CREDITS

170 "**Dans mon village** . . . **every bush**" French song, unknown author, English translation by Anam Zafar and Sophie Lewis.

188 "**Le matin** . . . **Allah**" "Zoubida," performed by Josephine Baker on her album *C'est Vous*. Honoré and Jean Tranchant © Éditions Beuscher Arpège, 1972.

NOTES

1. Article in *Candide* newspaper by Pierre de Régnier, translation by Anam Zafar and Sophie Lewis.

2. Quotation from *L'Ame et la Danse* (*Dance and the Soul*), by Paul Valéry, translated by Dorothy Bussy.

3. Michel Duran, source unknown, translation by Anam Zafar and Sophie Lewis.

4. Henry Bénazet, source unknown, translation by Anam Zafar and Sophie Lewis.

5. Alexandre Arnoux for *Les Nouvelles Littéraires*, translated by Anam Zafar and Sophie Lewis.

6. Jacques Abtey, *La Guerre Secrète de Joséphine Baker* (Paris-La Havane: Éditions Siboney, 1948).

7. Preface by Josephine Baker in Paul Colin's portfolio *Le Tumulte Noir* © Paris, Éditions d'Art, 1928. Preface originally written in English and has been lightly edited.

8. Jean Barreyre, unknown source, translated by Anam Zafar and Sophie Lewis.

9. Translators' note: While the original text says "64th Street," it may in fact refer to 63rd Street, as mentioned on p. 30–31.

10. Translators' note: This has been corrected to "west coast"; the original text described it as on the east coast.

11. Translators' note: "Alex" might refer to Joe Alex, a cast member in *Siren of the Tropics*.

12. "Minuit," bolero (Georges Tabet and Lull Michaelli—Jo Bouillon and Pierre Guillermin); "Revoir Paris," corrido (André Hornez and Jacques

Mareuil, Augustín Lara, Maria Bonita); "Olele Olela," marchinha (André Hornez, M. Salina, and Jo Bouillon); and "Bahiana," samba (George Negrette, Dorival Caymmi).

13. "Zoubida/Chanson Mauresque," by Jean Tranchant.

14. Extract from *Mon Sang dans Tes Veines* © Éditions Isis, Paris, 1931. Originally in French, English translation by Anam Zafar and Sophie Lewis.

15. Translators' note: The "four generals" are Winston Churchill, Franklin D. Roosevelt, Joseph Stalin, and Charles de Gaulle.

16. Charles Mason and Jeremiah Dixon established this line in 1768 after being commissioned by the heirs of William Penn and Lord Baltimore to settle a dispute over the boundary between Pennsylvania and Maryland.

ABOUT THE AUTHOR

Josephine Baker (1906–1975) was an entertainer, World War II spy, and civil rights activist. Born in St. Louis, Missouri, she performed on Broadway as a teenager during the Harlem Renaissance and sailed to Paris in 1925, at the age of nineteen. She became a star there as a dancer and singer, headlining across Europe and achieving international celebrity. In 1927, she became the first Black woman to star in a major motion picture. She joined the French intelligence agency during World War II, serving as a spy for the French Resistance and earning honors for her valor and bravery. In the 1960s and '70s, she joined the civil rights movement, and in 1963 she spoke at the March on Washington alongside Martin Luther King Jr. In later life, she adopted twelve children. She passed away in 1975. In 2021, Baker became the first Black woman to enter France's Panthéon.